ɪb of ‘Abdullāh Anṣārī, in Gāzar-gāh of Herāt. This entrance to ɪe was reconstructed in 1428, at the order of Shāh Rūkh, by an t named Zain-ud-din, who so revered Anṣārī that he asked to be acing the shrine, with his tombstone in the form of a kneeling dog. ɔe seen in the left of the plate above.

Masatoshi Konishi, 1967

Th
the
arc
bur
It n

Pho

‘ABDULLĀH ANṢĀRĪ OF HERĀT
(1006-1089 C.E.)
An Early Ṣūfi Master

CURZON SUFI SERIES

Series Editor:
Ian Richard Netton
Professor of Arabic Studies, University of Leeds

The *Curzon Sufi Series* attempts to provide short introductions to a variety of facets of the subject, which are accessible both to the general reader and the student and scholar in the field. Each book will be either a synthesis of existing knowledge or a distinct contribution to, and extension of, knowledge of the particular topic. The two major underlying principles of the Series are sound scholarship and readability.

AL-HALLAJ

Herbert W. Mason

PERSIAN SUFI POETRY
An Introduction to the Mystical Use of Classical Persian Poetry

J.T.P. de Bruijn

RUZBIHAN BAQLI
Mysticism and the Rhetoric of Sainthood in Persian Sufism

Carl W.Ernst

BEYOND FAITH AND INFIDELITY
The Sufi Poetry and Teachings of Mahmud Shabistari

Leonard Lewisohn

‘ABDULLĀH ANṢĀRĪ OF HERĀT (1006-1089 C.E.)

An Early Ṣūfi Master

A. G. Ravân Farhâdi

Formerly Professor at Sorbonne Nouvelle, Paris and at the University of California, Berkeley

CURZON
PRESS

First published in 1996
by Curzon Press
St John's Studios, Church Road, Richmond
Surrey, TW9 2QA

Typeset in Baskerville by Excel Books, New Delhi
Printed in Great Britain by
Biddles Limited, Guildford and King's Lynn

British Library Cataloguing in Publication Data
A catalogue record for this book is available from the British Library

Library of Congress in Publication Data
A catalog record for this book has been requested

ISBN 0 7007 0313 6

CONTENTS

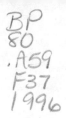

LIST OF TABLES AND APPENDIXES

TRANSLITERATIONS

Consonants

th	ث
ḥ	ح
kh	خ
dh	ذ
sh	ش
ṣ	ص
ḍ	ض
ṭ	ط
ẓ	ظ
ʿ	ع
gh	غ
q	ق

Vowels

For Arabic Words:	For Persian Words:
a (fatḥa)	a
u (ḍamma)	o
i (kasra)	e
ā	ā
ū	ō, ū
ī	ē, ī
aw / au	aw / au
ay / ai	ay / ai

Persian Consonants

p	پ
ch	چ
g	گ

Dates

The Christian Era (C.E.) year is given after the lunar Hijra (H) year, e.g. "396/1006"

The tomb of 'Abdullāh Anṣārī in Gāzar-gāh of Herāt. Behind the tomb, a "Rawāq" (half dome) is decorated with glazed tile (kāshi) with calligraphic writing of Quranic verses.

Drawing by A. Shakūr Farhādi

PREFACE

Seventy-two years ago, Vladimir Ivanov wrote "The Ṭabaqāt of Anṣārī in the Old Language of Herāt" (*Journal of the Royal Asiatic Society,* January 1923). His article concentrated on the linguistic aspects, rather than on Sufism. It was sixty-one years ago that Hellmut Ritter became the first Western scholar to provide major information (in the German language) on the Ṣūfī works of Anṣārī in his article, "Philologika VII: Anṣārī Herewī..." (*Der Islam* 22: 1934). More recently, in 1965, Serge de Beaurecueil published (in French) a very fine study of Anṣārī and his works. He also offered a critical edition of *The Stations of the Wayfarers* (Manāzil al-Sāyirīn), which is the masterpiece of Anṣārī in Arabic, together with a translation into French (see Bibliography).

As no major study on 'Abdullāh Anṣārī of Herāt has been available in the English language, this short work has been written with the intention of filling the gap. I earnestly hope it will be followed by other works on Anṣārī in the English language.

The selections from Anṣārī translated herein involve many subtleties of Sufism, the mystical dimension of Islām. The reader who is unfamiliar with basic Ṣūfī teachings is therefore advised to read one of the many introductory books on Sufism published in the English language (see Bibliography).

ACKNOWLEDGMENTS

I am grateful to all those who have provided me with assistance in preparing this brief work:

Dr. Ibrāhīm Gamard deserves particular recognition. He is an American who has devoted himself to early Ṣūfī works in Persian and with whom I have been working since 1986 in preparing the annotated English translation of the "Rubā'iyāt" (Quatrains) of Mawlānā Jalāl-ud-dīn of Balkh (called "Rūmī"). He did the preliminary, and later, the final editing of this book (typing it onto computer disk together with transliteration signs), which included some very helpful rewriting. Without his scholarly and generous contribution, this book would not have been ready for publication.

I am very thankful to Dr. Leonard Lewisohn of the Center of Near Eastern Studies, SOAS, University of London, for having suggested valuable proposals for the improvement of the translation of many passages of *The Hundred Grounds* (Sad Maydān) of Anṣārī.

My brother, 'Abd-ul-Shakūr Farhādī, a professor of Architecture (in Greenville, North Carolina), offered his drawing of the shrine surrounding the tomb of 'Abdullāh Anṣārī (in Gāzar-gāh, located in a suburb of Herāt). His son, Adīb Farhādī typed major parts of the book. Other parts were first typed by Jān-Aḥmad Taymūree. In the later stages of the work, I had the helpful cooperation of Nāhīd Fārūq and Shahīra Shair.

I am glad to have had, while in Paris in September 1993, an interesting exchange of views about the contents of this book with my friend of 42 years, Serge de Laugier de Beaurecueil. He has spent a good part of his life studying the life and works of Anṣārī, and had, for many years, made Afghānistān his second home country (see Bibliography).

I am grateful to Professor Ḥāmid Algar, who has been my colleague for many years in the Department of Near Eastern Studies at the University of California, Berkeley, for encouraging me to work on this book. He made available to me his ten volumes of the "Kashf al-Asrār," a commentary on the Qur'ān in Persian which is based on the teachings of 'Abdullāh Anṣārī.

I am also grateful to Dr. Ian Richard Netton of the Department of Arabic and Islamic Studies, University of Exeter, England, and to Martina Campbell of Curzon Press for having asked me to write this book.

'Abd-ul-Ghafūr Ravān FARHĀDĪ
United Nations, New York
1995

PART ONE

AN OUTLINE OF

THE LIFE OF

‘ABDULLĀH ANṢĀRĪ OF HERĀT

(1006-1089 C.E.)

SOURCES FOR HIS BIOGRAPHY

In studying the history of the life of 'Abdullāh Anṣārī of Herāt, we are fortunate to have some excellent sources available in Arabic and Persian:

1. The *Appendices to the Generations of Hanbalites* (Ḍayl'alā Ṭabaqāt al-Ḥanābila) by Ibn Rajab of Baghdād (D. 796/1393)[1] provides important material in Arabic on the life history of Anṣārī.
2. The *Characters of Great and Prominent People* (Siyar al-A'lām al-Nubalā') by Al-Dhahabī[2] also contains interesting information in Arabic.
3. The *Breezes of Intimacy* (Nafaḥāt al-Uns) by Mawlānā 'Abd-al-Raḥmān Jāmī of Herāt (817-898/1414-1492)[3], contains an important chapter on Anṣārī in Persian. The text also includes a summary of a pamphlet written by Jāmī, "The Records and Acts of the Senior-of-Islam 'Abdullāh Anṣārī" (Manāqib-é Shaykh al-Islām 'Abdullāh Anṣārī). The full text of the "Records" was edited by the late Professor A.J. Arberry.[4] The "Records" are mainly autobiographical, in that they are based on the notes of novices who wrote the material based on the narrations of their old master Anṣārī about his memories of childhood and early youth. (See: *Nafaḥāt* p.336 to 355.

We do not need to repeat here all the references to the above mentioned sources. Serge de Laugier de Beaurecueil has provided detailed references to these sources in his *Khwāja 'Abdullāh Anṣārī, Mystique Hanbalite.*[5]

The large amount of precisely dated events of Anṣārī's life available to us, especially in the work of Ibn Rajab, allows us to make a good chronology of his life. There are very few great figures who lived many centuries ago about whom there is so much accurate information.

His Genealogy, Name, and Titles

Anṣārī's genealogy can be found in the earliest manuscripts of his works:

1. 'Abdullāh Abū-Ismā'īl Anṣārī, son of
2. Muḥammad Abū-Manṣūr Anṣārī, son of
3. 'Alī Abū-Ma'ād Anṣārī, son of
4. Aḥmad Anṣārī, son of
5. 'Alī Anṣārī, son of
6. Ja'far Anṣārī, son of
7. Manṣūr Anṣārī, son of
8. Abū-Manṣūr Mat Anṣārī, son of
9. Abū-Ayyūb Khālid ibn Zayd al-Khazrajī al-Najjārī al-Azdī.

His family name derives from the Anṣār ("Helpers"), who were Muslim citizens of Yathrīb, the Arabian city later named "Madīnah," who generously helped the Prophet and his Meccan followers, the Muḥājir ("Immigrants"), to establish themselves in 622 C.E. and during the subsequent decade.

Abū-Ayyūb had taken charge of the Prophet's journey, and was afterwards called the "Companion in Charge of the Camel Saddle" (Ṣāḥib al-Raḥl). The Prophet honored him by staying first in his house after arriving in Yathrīb. Abū-Ayyūb later took part in battles against the armies of Rūm (Byzantium). His son, Abū-Manṣūr Mat al-Anṣārī, came to Herāt during the Caliphate of 'Uthmān (23-35/644-656) in the company of Aḥnaf Ibn Qays, the Arab expedition leader who conquered Herāt (in 31/652). Abū-Manṣūr Mat and his successive descendants seem to have generally lived in Herāt until 'Abdullāh Anṣārī was born in 396/1006.

The name "Khwāja," which often precedes Anṣārī's name in Persian writings, means "Master" (and was a term used by Ferdawsī in his Shāh-Nāma, c.a. 1000 C.E.). It was traditional, and still is, for descendants of the major companions of the Prophet living in Persian-speaking lands to be addressed by this honorific title. It will not be used in this book, and it is not used in the Arabic sources.

The name "Hirawī," or "Harawī," is an Arabic name meaning "belonging to Heray" or "Harī," the early name of Herāt (the final *āt* is an Arabic ending plural form). "Herāt" means "Harī and its countryside." (Other place names near Herāt have a similar construction, such as "Ghōrāt" and "Badghēsāt"). It is important to remember that Anṣārī's Arab biographers wrote his last name as "al-Hirawī" (or "al-Harawī"), rather than "Anṣārī." The English form, "of Herāt," is used here since it expresses better the meaning of "Hirawī."

The ancient name of Herāt is "Harayva" (Avestan, Old Persian). Its Middle Persian name was "Hérév." In early Islamic times, the name of the city was pronounced "Haré" and "Héré." "Harawī" or "Hérawī/Hirawī" is an Arabicized form meaning "belonging to Haré."

His title, "Shaykh al-Islām" ("The Senior of Islām"), was recorded in the decree of the 'Abbāsīd Caliph al-Qā'im in 462/1070. This title is often used by authors who quote Anṣārī. The decree also contained the titles "Shaykh al-Shuyūkh" ("Senior of the Seniors") and "Zayn al-'Ulamā" ("Ornament of the Scholars"). He was also given the title "Nāṣir al-Sunnah" ("Supporter of the Prophetic Tradition").

'Abū-l-Faḍl al-Maybodī, the author of "Kashf al-Asrār" (see the preliminary notes on this work), often calls Anṣārī "Pīr-é Ṭarīqat" ("Shaykh of the Path") when quoting his Ṣūfī commentaries.

The title "Pīr-é Herāt" (the Shaykh of Herāt") was later used in Persian texts.

The name " 'Abdullāh" ("Servant of God"), is more correctly written as " 'Abd-Allāh," but it is written here according to the common transliteration in English. His surname (kunyat), "Abū-Ismā'īl," is rarely used in common quotations. In the time of Anṣārī, this kind of name was still formally given to male children in Persian-speaking lands, but later seems to have become omitted in spoken language. Eventually this practice was abandoned in Persian-speaking countries, as well as in Turkish-speaking ones.

Stages of His Life

"I belong to the spring, the season of flowers
and sweet smelling plants (rayāḥin)."

A) Ages 1 to 10: Childhood (1006 - 1016 C.E.):

'Abdullāh Anṣārī was born in Herāt on the evening of May 4, 1006 C.E. (Sha'bān 2, 396 H). He said, "I was born in the Old Citadel

(Kohan-dezh). I have grown up there, (and) no other place has been dearer to me." (Quoted by Jāmi in Manāqib)

His father, Abū-Manṣūr, was a shop keeper in the "Old Citadel" district and was a Ṣūfī. He had spent many years of his youth in Balkh, first as the disciple of Abū-l-Muẓaffar Ḥabbāl of Termēz, an ascetic Ṣūfī of the Hanbalite school. After that, he became a disciple of Sharīf Ḥamza 'Aqīlī of Termēz, who lived in Balkh in the company of Sufis that were following the Baghdad traditions (of the "Junayd" school of Sufism). When Abū-Manṣūr returned to Herāt, he started a family. He remained a scrupulous and dedicated Ṣūfī, and associated with the Ṣūfī masters of Herāt.

'Abdullāh was put in a school that was taught by a woman. Then he attended the Mālīnī school. By age six he learned the reading of the Qur'ān taught to him by the school "readers" (muqri'). At the age of nine, his father and a teacher named Jārūdī began to dictate Traditions (aḥādīth — sayings of the Prophet) to him.

However, about this time his father suddenly abandoned his family and shop, and left Herāt to look for his former Ṣūfi companions in Balkh.

B) Ages 11 to 19: A Precocious Teenager (1017 - 1025 C.E.):

'Abdullāh continued his studies, which by age eleven included the study of poetry under a "well-read scholar" (adīb). His daily practice was to study and memorize passages from the Qur'ān and Traditions, and to write letters and poetry. He studied so hard at home that he hardly allowed himself time to eat ("my mother put cooked spinach in my mouth"). Still abandoned by the father, the family remained destitute, but helped by some friends.

From the ages of thirteen to sixteen 'Abdullāh had four significant teachers:

(1) A Ṣūfī named Shaykh 'Amū, who had met many Sufis (including 'Ab-ul-'Abbās Nahāwandī) during his extensive travels, and who also had built a Ṣūfī convent (khānaqāh) in a suburb of Herāt. When 'Abdullāh was only fourteen, the shaykh appointed him to be his successor.

(2) An explainer of the Qur'ān named Yaḥyā Ibn 'Ammār Shaybānī, who was an opponent of the Ash'arī philosophers (whom he called "innovators" — ahl-é bid'at).

(3) 'Abdul-Jabbār Jarrāḥī, who taught him Traditions from the *Collection* (Jāmi') of Tirmidhī.

(4) Ṭāqī of Sejestān, a sensitive and penetrating Ṣūfī master who began teaching him in his adolescence and who told him, "O 'Abdullāh, praise be to God! What a light He has put in your heart!"

From the ages of seventeen to nineteen he continued his studies of the Qur'ān and Traditions and also continued to be exposed and initiated into different levels of the Ṣūfī path.

C) Ages 20 to 27: Toward Maturity (1026 - 1033 C.E.):

At the age of twenty, his spiritual mentor, Ṭāqī died, and 'Abdullāh went to the city of Nishāpūr to further study Traditions and to meet well-known Ṣūfī masters such as Abū-Naṣr Manṣūr Aḥmad al-Mufassir, Abū-Sa'īd Sayrafī, and Abū-l-Ḥasan Aḥmad Salīṭī. He avoided contacts with those who were influenced by Ash'arite philosophy, which included Abū-l-Qāsim al-Qushayrī (d. 1072), the author of the famous *Treatise* (Risāla) on Sufism.

During the next year he was quite active in Herāt in the meetings of the scholars of the Traditions. Then, at age twenty-two, Shaykh 'Amū made him the director of his Ṣūfī convent in Herāt. Anṣārī's teacher of Quranic commentary, Yaḥyā b. 'Ammār Shaybānī, died several years later (in 1031).

When Anṣārī was twenty-six, in 1032, he offered to accompany the elderly Imām Abū-l-Faḍl b. Sa'd of Herāt to Mecca for the Pilgrimage (Ḥajj). However, when the caravan reached Baghdād, it had to return to Khorāsān because of news that the roads between Irāq and the Hijāz in Arabia were too dangerous. By the spring of 1032, he was back in Herāt.

He tried again the next year. While staying in Nishāpūr at the Ṣūfī convent of Ibn Bākū, he met the famous Ṣūfī Abū-Sa'īd b. Abū-l-Khayr, who told him about the Ṣūfī master, Kharaqānī. He then went with a caravan that brought him again into Irāq, to the city of Rayy. However, once again, the lack of security forced the caravan to return to Khorāsān. While staying in the town of Dāmghān, Anṣārī met another famous Ṣūfī, Muḥammad Qaṣṣāb of Āmol. And on his way back home from there, he met the extraordinary Kharaqānī, an encounter which transformed his life (see section below on "His Meeting with Kharaqānī").

D) Ages 28 to 35: Beginning Years of Teaching (1034 - 1041):

By November 1033, Anṣārī was back in Herāt and living in the Ṣūfī convent (khānaqāh) of Shaykh 'Amū. Later during that winter (in 1034), Anṣārī spent some ecstatic days during a meeting of Sufis in Nobādhān, south of Herāt. As a result of that meeting, he decided to cease participating in Ṣūfī gatherings engaged in music and ecstatic movements — the "spiritual concert" (samā'). He chose to commit himself to a Sufism of sobriety and lucidity (ṣaḥw), rather than the delirious and frenzied kind.

The following year, he made a visit to Ṣūfī shaykhs in the town of Chesht, at the upper Harī-rōd (river) basin.

In the year 1038, his teacher of Traditions, Abū-Ya'qūb, died and Anṣārī took charge of the teaching. That same year he was summoned to the court of Sulṭān Mas'ūd in Herāt.

The following year, Anṣārī's father died in Balkh. In 1039, Anṣārī was again summoned to the court of the Sultan, accused by the Ash'arites of teaching anthropomorphism (tashbīh). The Sultan was reassured of the soundness of his teaching and he received honors.

Around the year 1040, at the age of 34, Anṣārī wrote *Forty Traditions on the Divine Unity* (al-Arba'īn fī Dalā'il al-Tawḥīd).

E) Ages 36 to 46: A decade of Hardships (1042 - 1052 C.E.):

Two years later, in 1041, he was prohibited from teaching by an assembly of theologians. Anṣārī exiled himself to the town of Shakīwān, near Pōshanj until the year 1043.

By the year of 1044, at the age of 38, he returned to Herāt and re-started his teaching of Quranic commentary.

In 1046, another assembly of theologians presented a petition against Anṣārī, and he was banished from Herāt and imprisoned (with chains) during five months in Pōshanj.

Two years later, he was again back in Herāt and resuming his Quranic commentary. During this period, he spent large amounts of time teaching the interpretation of the second chapter of the Qur'an, verses 160-65, about those who are "the most ardent in their love of God." On November 30, 1049, Shaykh 'Amū died. After that, Anṣārī lived at home in extreme poverty. Since he was well-dressed while teaching, his friends were unaware of his indigence.

F) Ages 47 to 57: A Decade of Achievements (1053 - 1063 C.E.):

By the year 1053, at the age of 47, Anṣārī's reputation had spread all over the Seljukid and Abbassid Empires. He was visited by Abūl-Ḥasan of Bākharz and Abūl-Qāsim al-Bāri' of Zōzan.

By the following year, his friends became aware of his poverty at home and began making gifts to him. In 1055, a Hanafite judge, Abū-l-'Alā Sa'īd b. Sayyār, offered Anṣārī a place in the major mosque of Herāt in order to teach Quranic commentary and to preach.

At the age of 50, in the years 1056-57, Anṣārī dictated "The Hundred Grounds" (Sad Maydān), a mnemonic Ṣūfī manual in Darī-Persian, to one of his students.

In 1059, some of his opponents made an unsuccessful petition (to the Seljuk leader, Alp Arslān) to prohibit him from lecturing.

During these years, in his fifties, friends and students supported him and his economic situation improved. He said, "God has never found me, even for half a day, hunting for the wealth of this world....Friends, themselves, are offering me so many of the things that I desired during earlier times....Yet, although it were the kingdom of Solomon, all this would be now meaningless to me!"

G) Ages 58 to 64: Combating the Innovators (1064 - 1070 C.E.):

In 1064, Anṣārī's opponents tried to provoke a polemic with him in the presence of the Sultan, Alp Arslān, and his Vizier, Niẓām al-Mulk, but Anṣārī refused to discuss anything that was not based on the Qur'an and the Tradition (Sunnah).

Two years later, his opponents succeeded in obtaining an expulsion order against him from the Vizier. Anṣārī was exiled to Balkh for a short time, and then was given permission to return to Herāt.

The Vizier subsequently amended his policy and adopted a policy in favor of the traditionalists. (Anṣārī had refused a robe of honor sent to him by the Vizier, after an opponent named Dabūsī asked him uncourtly questions about Ash'arite philosophy in the presence of the Vizier, and Anṣārī took umbrage and left the meeting). By the year 1068, Anṣārī continued to preach in the Grand Mosque of Herāt and to teach Quranic commentary. And he continued to guide the novices in the Ṣūfī convent (khānaqāh).

During the next year, his opponents made a failed attempt to accuse him of anthropomorphism in the presence of the Sultan, and later in the same year (1069), Anṣārī was sent a robe of honor from Baghdād from the Caliph al-Qā'im (on the suggestion of Niẓām al-Mulk).

H) Ages 65 to 78: Celebrity and Grandeur (1071 - 1084 C.E.):

In 1071, it was recorded that Marzūq Mu'tamin Sājī and Muḥammad b. Ṭāhir were two of his close associates in the Ṣūfī convent.

At the age of 66, the next year, Anṣārī suffered a severe illness, but recovered. His eyesight was constantly weakening.

During his late sixties and seventies, Anṣārī continued to teach Traditions (aḥādīth), Quranic commentary (tafsīr), and Sufism. However, in 473/1080, at the age of 74, Anṣārī *became blind.*

I) Ages 79 to 82: The Battles of the Last Years (1085 - 1088 C.E.):

Subsequent to his blindness, Anṣārī continued to dictate Quranic commentary and Ṣūfī teachings. Some of his young students, such as 'Abd-al-Awwal Sejzī, 'Abd-al-Mālik Karrokhī and Muḥammad Ṣayadalānī, served as his scribes. During this period his secretary, Ḥusayn Kotobī, took care of his everyday life affairs. In the year 1082, Anṣārī dictated "The Stations of the Wayfarers" (Manāzil al-Sā'irīn), the famous Ṣūfī manual in Arabic, to his young novices. And during the same year, the Caliph al-Muqtadī sent Anṣārī a robe of honor and gave him the title, "Shaykh al-Islām" (the "Senior of Islam"). In December 1085 (Ramadhān 478), Anṣārī severely criticized a scholar of scholastic rationalism (Kalām) who had come to Herāt. Anṣārī's followers burnt down the scholar's house and beat him. As a result, Anṣārī and his companions were exiled and ordered to go to Balkh.

The next year, at age 80 (on April 21, 1087), Anṣārī was triumphantly welcomed back to Herāt, where he continued to teach Quranic commentary.

On Friday, March 8, 1089 (22 Ḏẖū'l-Ḥijja 481), 'Abdullāh Anṣārī of Herāt died, at the age of 82. He was buried on a rainy day at Gāzar-gāh, near the Ṣūfī convent and the tomb of Shaykh 'Amū. Since then, Anṣārī's tomb became a major shrine visited by pilgrims.

SPECIAL TOPICS CONCERNING HIS LIFE

His Hanbalism

'Abdullāh Anṣārī of Herāt was a great figure in the Ḥanbalī school of Sunnī Islām. And it is through Ḥanbalī biographers that we have received such detailed and precise information about Anṣārī. One of his masters of early youth, Ṭāqi Sejestāni was a Ḥanbalī.

There are many common points between the lives of the Imām Ibn Ḥanbal (164-241/780-855) and Anṣārī. Both spent their childhoods in poverty and experienced indigence during many years of their adulthoods. Both were diligent students of Traditions (aḥādīṯẖ) first, and then became prominent teachers of this subject. Both vehemently opposed the rationalistic views of the philosophers (the Muʿtazilites, in the case of Ibn Ḥanbal; the Ashʿarites, in the case of Anṣārī). Both believed that the Word of God (the Qurʾān) is pre-eternal (qadīm) and not "created" (makẖlūq). Both were persecuted by those in power and showed great steadfastness during the trials and hardships (miḥnat) imposed upon them because of their beliefs. They never compromised with their doctrinal opponents, and neither engaged in duplicity of any kind.

It is clear that Anṣārī considered Ibn Ḥanbal to be a model. And the panegyric "Couplets" (qaṣīda — the one which ends with the letter "nūn"), composed in Arabic by Anṣārī was well-known to the Hanbalites. The following is an excerpt from this poem:

"I am a Hanbalite, while living and dying.
This is my testament, O brothers, to you!"[6]

Anṣārī quotes Ibn Ḥanbal as saying, "Knowledge (maʿrifat — of God) is not 'created' (makẖlūq), because the created cannot attain to the Creator."[7] Anṣārī also reports that: "Once, the great Ṣūfī master Abū-Ḥamza of Baghdād (d. 289/902) was in the presence of

Aḥmad Ibn Ḥanbal. Someone asked a question. Ibn Ḥanbal said to Abū-Ḥamza: 'O Ṣūfī, give the answer!" (ajib, yā Ṣūfī)."[8] Anṣārī is careful to remind the novices about the great Ṣūfī masters who were Hanbalites.[9] The Hanbalism of Anṣārī is based on the main principle that the Qur'an and the Tradition (Sunnah — of the Prophet) are the basic sources of religious sciences. Anṣārī's Sufism is also based on this principle, since he views Sufism as an integral part of Islam. One cannot be a wayfarer (sāyir) toward God without being a good Muslim believer. Anṣārī blames the Ash'arites ("who do not know even a single ḥadīth") by saying, "They consider the followers of the Sunnah (Tradition) to be deprived of (religious) knowledge!"

In reading "A Supplement to the Generations of Hanbalites" (Dhayl 'Ala Ṭabaqāt al-Ḥanābila) by Ibn Rajab Baghdādi (d. 795/1393),[10] we find that these biographers expressed great respect for the Ṣūfī Hanbalites. Ibn Rajab's work is a valuable source on the biography of 'Abdullāh Anṣārī of Herāt.

A new school of Hanbalism was founded by Ibn Taimiyya (661-728/1263-1328). He was a literalist (accused of being anthropomorphist) who wrote against the Sufi masters (particularly Ibn 'Arabī) and called them "innovators" (ahl al-bid'a). He was a forerunner of the more recent Salafī movement, which is also critical of Ṣūfī congregations, and sometimes of Sufism in general. Salafī scholars have not belonged only to the Hanbalite school, but to the other three schools of Sunnism as well. Ibn Qayyim al-Jawziyya (d. 1350 C.E.), in his "Book of the Secrets of Prayer" (Kitāb Asrār al-Ṣalāt), includes a Ṣūfī interpretation of prayer, saying, "He is the Most High Who praises Himself through the tongue of the praising one..."[11] In spite of the critical tenor of his commentary on Anṣārī's "Stations of the Wayfarers" (Manāzil al-Sāyarīn), he does not seem to be systematically anti-Ṣūfī or anti-Anṣārī. According to Ibn Qayyim, the "Station" is useful in so far as it facilitates the understanding of the spiritual itinerary for the journey toward God. Ibn Qayyim believes in the stages, grades, and stations of the journey which are based on Quranic texts. He cannot be called an opponent of Sufism, but can be viewed as a "severe interpreter" of it. His bulky "Grades of the Wayfarers" (Madārij al-Sālikīn) deserves a general analysis.[12]

Muḥammad Ibn 'Abd-al-Wahhāb (1115-1201/1703-1787), the

founder of Wahhabism, gave a new dimension to the austere aspects of Ibn Taymiyya's doctrines. Wahhabism considers many Ṣūfī beliefs and practices to be objectionable innovations (bid'a). As the majority of Hanbalites (in Arabia and the Gulf region) are now followers of Wahhabism (sometimes called the "Salafī" way), the great traditional figures of Hanbalism who respected Sufism are no longer considered as deserving the attention of researchers. The official media and popular publications in the countries concerned are silent about those great Hanbalite figures of Sunnī Islām who were also great Sūfis.

However, the Persian-speaking Sunnis and Shī'a admire Anṣārī because of his "Intimate Invocations" (Munājāt). Shī'a intellectuals also greatly appreciate Anṣārī's other works. The ten volumes of his Quranic commentary (Kashf al-Asrār), written in Darī-Persian, continue to be reprinted in Tehrān, the capital of a country where Shī'a are the majority. But most Arabic-speaking Muslims, and many Urdu-speaking Shī'a seem to be unaware of the great significance of Anṣārī's works.

His Meeting with Kharaqānī

In 424/1033, when he was 27 years old, while returning from Rayy, 'Abdullāh Anṣārī met Abū-l-Ḥasan Kharaqānī, an encounter which deeply affected his life. Kharaqānī was an elderly and illiterate Ṣūfī master who read into the heart of Anṣārī and answered even his unspoken and unformulated questions.

Anṣārī later said, "If I hadn't met Kharaqānī, I would never have known the Reality (Ḥaqīqat). He said to me, 'The one who eats and sleeps is someone else.' When I heard this, I myself was Kharaqānī." While talking to Anṣārī, Kharaqānī went into ecstasies and burst into tears.[13] This meeting was an instance of spiritual communication. An event which happened most probably a short time after this encounter, shows an evolution in Anṣārī's approach to Sufism:

Aḥmad of Chesht and Abū-Sa'īd Mu'allim, two Sufis, were engaged in a fierce dispute, about whether it is better to be a seeker (murīd) of God or one who is sought (murād) by God. They asked Anṣārī to arbitrate. His verdict was overwhelming: "There is no seeker, no sought, no receiving of information, no inquiry, no definition, and no description! He (God) is everything in every-

Table A

The Place of Anṣārī in the Historical Development of Hanbalism

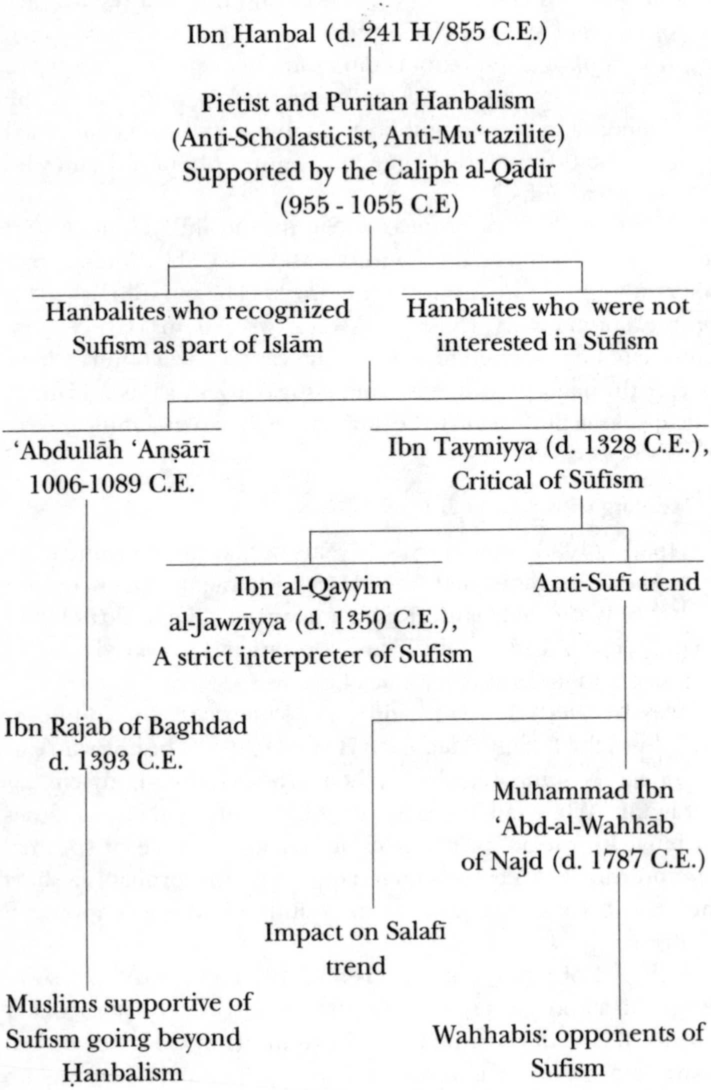

thing!"

Anṣārī, however, did not choose the kind of Sufism which emphasizes the seeking of ecstatic experiences. This is demonstrated by what happened to him during the Ṣūfī meeting he attended in Nobā<u>dh</u>ān (near Herāt and now called Nawbādām) when he was 28 years old.[14] He had participated in the "spiritual concert" (samā') and tore his shirt in a moment of ecstasy. And he was very much venerated by the sixty-two Sufis present in that gathering and was offered many gifts. His response was to hurriedly leave the meeting, without taking the gifts, and to return to Herāt. He had become sharply aware of the dangers of being overly revered by others and of being attached to seeking ecstasy.

NOTES TO PART I

1. Damascus, 1951.
2. Cairo (n.d.).
3. Tehrān, 1991.
4. *Islamic Quarterly,* 1963, pp. 57-82.
5. Beirut, 1965.
6. See Aḥmad <u>Sh</u>arabāṣī, "al-A'imma al-Arba'a," Beirut.
7. "Ṭabaqāt al-Ṣūfiyya," Mawlāyi edition, p. 463.
8. "Ṭabaqāt al-Ṣūfiyya," p. 148.
9. Also in "Ṭabaqāt al-Ṣūfiyya."
10. This is a "supplement" to Ibn Abi-Ya'lā's "The Generations of Hanbalites" (Ṭabaqāt al-Ḥanābila).
11. See Schimmel, 1975, p. 164.
12. Edited by Ra<u>sh</u>īd Riḍā in 3 volumes in 1334/1914; new edition, Cairo, 1956.
13. Anṣārī has himself given a description of his brief encounter with <u>Kh</u>araqānī. See in the Bibliography: Ed. Arberry, 1963; and the "Nafaḥāt" of Jāmī, edited by Maḥmūd 'Abedī, Tehrān, 1991. (pp. 336-346).
14. Mentioned in the previous section on the "Outline" of Anṣārī's life. See also pages 139, 140.

PART TWO

SELECTIONS FROM

THE WORKS OF

‘ABDULLĀH ANṢĀRĪ OF HERĀT

1006-1089 CE

INTRODUCTION

'Abdullāh Anṣārī of Herāt is considered a "great writer." and yet he almost never wrote! Most of his works that are available to us are based on the notes of students and novices, notes which he rarely checked or edited (including the "Manāzil al-Sāyirīn"). In some cases, a work was expanded by a scholar (such as the "Kashf al-Asrār," the commentary and exegesis of the Qur'an); in other cases a work was left in the form of crude "notes de cours" (as with the "Ṭabaqāt al-Ṣūfiyya").

Anṣārī was more a teacher who lectured than a penner who wrote. His training as a student and later as a teacher of Traditions (ahādīth), enhanced by his prodigious memory, enabled him to speak like a book. He was the first to prepare short mnemonic treatises on very complicated and difficult subjects of Sūfism. These treatises strikingly resemble (in form, but not substance), twentieth century "résumé aide-mémoire" manuals of students of the "humanities" that are meticulously prepared for taking frightening entry examinations. Such is the case of the "Hundred Grounds" (Sad Maydān) and the "Stations of Wayfarers" (Manāzil al-Sāyirīn).

In this introduction, we offer a presentation, in our sections, of his books, treatises, and minor works, and a listing of Persian works attributed to him in the manuscripts of the 15th century and later (but not authenticated by the early manuscripts). However, in the latter case, one cannot reject these later manuscripts outright, because some of their contents can be substantially traced to early manuscripts. An example of this is the "Treatise on the Heart and Soul" (Risāla-yé Del-o Jān) found only in a 15th century manuscript.[1] It contains part of the text, or a paraphrase, of what we read in two pages from the "Commentary on the Qur'an" (Kashf al-Asrār).[2] In a general way, many parts of the texts found in the 15th century manuscripts can also be traced in earlier manuscripts (such as the "Kashf al-Asrār" and the "Ṭabaqāt"; see pages 115 to 117).

On the other hand, the factors weighing against the possibility that the treatises in later manuscripts are the works of Anṣārī (and are, therefore, the works of others) are the following:

1. The habit of some scribes, especially calligraphers (who in this case would have lived in the 15th century C.E.), of copying the manuscript of a Ṣūfī treatise which lacked the author's name on it, and attributing it (perhaps in good faith) to a famous figure. A similar factor could be the temptation of some authors to seek fame for their own manuscripts by attributing them to the great Anṣārī.
2. The tendency of some writers to become imitators of famous authors. Some may have written, in good faith, their own treatises or "intimate invocations" (munājāt) for some reason in the style of Anṣārī, while plagiarizing to some degree, but refrained from writing their own names. Some of them may have written their own names at the end of a work, but the last folio was torn away or damaged so as to become illegible. Such a collection could have been attributed to Anṣārī by a scribe or calligrapher of a later generation, after the imitating author (not well-known) had died. Such a scribe or calligrapher might have lived in a far away city and wanted the fame of "discovering" or "owning" a work of Anṣārī. Or the motive might have been, in the case of genuine fraud, to obtain material gain by selling the treatises or "intimate invocations" to amateur collectors or to prominent figures such as rulers, dignitaries, or wealthy persons.

All the works of Anṣārī did not have the same fortune. Among Arab scholars, and those using Arabic as their only means for studying Sufism, he was known only for his "Stations of the Wayfarers" (Manāzil al-Sāyirīn) and by the name of "Harawī" (the "Herāti"). S. de Laugier de Beaurecueil[3] has made a concise analysis of all the major commentaries in Arabic from the 13th century C.E. to our time by famous authors such as 'Abdul Mu'ṭī al-Iskandarī, 'Abd-al-Razzāq al-Qāshānī, Shams al-Dīn Tustarī, and Ibn Qayyim al-Jawziyya. Only one major commentary is in Persian (by Shams al-Dīn Tabadakānī, in the 15th century).

Among Persian-speaking peoples, and those who know Persian, scholars study the "Ṭabaqāt" and the "Kashf al-Asrār" (all published in the last decades). However, thousands of common readers only read the "Intimate Invocations" (Munājāt). Anṣārī, as in his day, continues to maintain a popular fame. During the last centuries, his celebrity and the continued popular attachment to him have become established facts. His admirers, many of whom are semi-literate and have never heard of the other works of the Master, can recite his ecstatic "Invocations" in Persian — while these works are unknown to Arab scholars, who know him only as austere Sufi master.

Table B

Books, Treatises and Minor Works of Anṣārī (d. 1089 C.E.) Found in Early Manuscripts and Quoted by His Earliest Biographers

I. WORKS ON FAITH, CREED AND SHARĪ'A

1. "Kashf al-Asrār" (in student notes for many years) in Darī-Persian	"Unveiling of the Secrets" (Commentary on the Qur'an) edited by Maybodī (d. 1126 C.E.)	Collected and published in ten volumes (1952, reprinted in 1960)
2. "Dham al-Kalām wa Ahl-ihi" in Arabic	"The Condemnation Of Scholastic Rationalism And Its Followers"	Manuscripts available, but not yet published
3. "Takfīr al-Jahmiyya" (Title mentioned in the "Dham al-Kalām")	"The Impiety of the Jahmites"	Manuscript not discovered
4. (Titles of Arabic treatises mentioned in other works of Anṣārī	A. "Forty Traditions (Aḥādīth) on the Attributes of (of God)" (Arba'īn fī Ṣifāt) B. "Forty Traditions (Aḥādīth) in the (Orthodox) Tradition (Arba'īn fī Sunnah)	The integral texts of some of these short treatises are not yet discovered

	C. "The Distinction Between the Attributes (of God)" (Al-Farūq fī Ṣifāt)	
	D. "The Fundamentals" (Al-Qawā'id)	
	E. "The Excellences of Ibn Ḥanbal" (Manāqib Aḥmad Ibn Ḥanbal)	

II. WORKS ON SUFISM

1. "Ṭabaquāt al-Ṣūfiyya" (in student notes for many years) in Darī-Persian	"The Generations of the Ṣūfis"	Published in one volume, of 968 pages, 1983

III. WORKS ON SPIRITUAL STAGES

1. "Sad Maydān" (1056 C.E.), in Darī-Persian	"The Hundred Grounds"	Published many times since 1954
2. "Manāzil al-Sāyirīn" (1082 C.E.), in Arabic	"The Stations of the Wayfarers"	Critical text published in 1962. Persian translation published in 1976
3. " 'Ilal al-Maqāmāt" (about 1085 C.E.), in Arabic	"The Flaws in the Stages"	Published in 1956
4. "Maqūlāt-o andarz-hā" (uttered at various times over many years) in Darī-Persian	"Sayings and Advice"	Incorporated in the "Kashf al-Asrār" and the "Ṭabaqāt"

IV. DEVOTIONAL INVOCATONS

1. "Munājāt" (uttered at various times over many years) in Darī-Persian	"Intimate Invocations"	Incorporated in the "Kashf al-Asrār" and in the "Ṭabaqāt"

Table C

Persian Works Attributed to Anṣārī in the Manuscripts of the 15th Century and Later But Not Authenticated by the Early Manuscripts

	Istanbul Manuscripts 1498 and 1500	Tehrān Manuscript 1500	Gonābādī Edition 1940	Shari'at Edition 1976	Helmut Ritter Listing, "Philologika" VII, 1934
[Kanz al-Sālikīn (Zād al-'Arifin)	X	X	X		X
Parda-ye Ḥejāb		X		X	
Su'āl-é Del az Jān		X	X	X	X
Qalandar Nāma		X	X	X	X
Maḥabbat Nāma		X	X		X
Wāridāt		X	X	X	X
Asrār Nāma					X
Ilāhi Nāma		X	X	X	
Munājāt	X	X			X
[Naṣīḥat (ba Niẓām-ul-Mulk)	X	X			X

NOTES

1. Pages 3 to 10 of Jawād Sharī'at's collection called "Sokhanān-é Pīr-é Herāt," 1982 edition.
2. Pages 59 and 60 of the first volume, 1960 edition.
3. Beaurecueil, "Chemin de Dieu," 1985, pp. 47-55.

COMMENTARY ON THE QUR'ĀN

(KASHF AL-ASRĀR)

BY 'ABDULLĀH ANṢĀRĪ OF HERĀT
(1006-1089 C.E.)

Edited by Rashīd al-Dīn Maybodī (d. 1126 C.E.)

Selected texts translated from the original Darī-Persian

PRELIMINARY NOTES

"I read the book, unique in its day and age, by Abū-Ismā'īl 'Abdullāh ibn Muḥammad ibn 'Alī Anṣāri, which is an exegesis and elucidation of the meanings of the Qur'an. Although I found it marvelously eloquent in syntax and expression and penetrating in its profundity and beauty, yet it was too succinct and concise. Thus, it hardly suited the purpose of students and wayfarers (on the Ṣūfī Path). Therefore, I undertook the task of providing a commentary and detailed exposition of its contents. It is an addition to "the realities of the commentary" (ḥaqā'iq al-tafsīr) and "the refinements of recalling (laṭā'if al-tadhkīr)." [—Written by Rashīd al-Dīn Maybodī (d. 520/1126), in the preface of "Kashf al-Asrār Wa 'Uddat al-Abrār" (Vol. I, p. 1, Tehrān, 1960 edition.]

Maybodī edited and expanded an earlier compilation of the commentary assembled by Anṣāri's disciples. The main teaching of Anṣāri during his career was Quranic commentary (tafsīr). As we found through studying his life, Anṣāri did not live long enough to finish the teaching of a very detailed exegesis of the Holy Book. The compilation edited by Maybodī[1] seems to come from a more concise commentary that Anṣāri taught. It was compiled by his students, whose names are not known to us in this connection.

"Kashf al-Asrār" (literally, "The Unveiling of the Secrets") is chronologically preceded by many translations of the Qur'an in Darī-Persian. Some of these translations were done under the Sāmānīds in Transoxiana and Khorāsān a century prior to the times of Anṣāri. Many of these (some published today, and others still in manuscript form) were supplemented by only some parts of Quranic commentary. Ṭabarī's commentary had already been translated into Darī-Persian (by the order of the Sāmānīds) in a summary form.

Therefore, "Kas͟hf al-Asrār" is the first systematic commentary on the Holy Book of Islām in Darī-Persian (and in any non-Arabic language as well). It summarizes, not only Ṭabarī's commentary, but also many other earlier Arabic commentaries of the Qur'an. Following after the "Ḥaqā'iq al-Tafsīr" of Abū-'Abd-al-Raḥmān Sulamī (of Nis͟hāpūr, d. 412/1021), a major (unpublished) Quranic commentary in Arabic with Ṣūfī teachings,[2] "Kas͟hf al-Asrār" is the earliest and most classical of Darī-Persian commentaries to be compiled, as based on the teaching of a great traditionalist and Ṣūfī master of Islām.

Long chapters of the Qur'an are covered in a number of chapters of commentary; but short chapters of the Qur'an constitute single chapters in the "Kas͟hf al-Asrār." Each chapter contains three different levels, or shifts (nawbat), each being a separate section:

Level 1: The Arabic Quranic text followed by Darī-Persian translation (which is very interesting not only to scholars of Quranic translations, but to researchers of early classical Darī-Persian phonetics, morphology and semantics).

Level 2: Common and exoteric commentary, covering major grammatical, historical, juridical, ethical and doctrinal matters, as well as general exegetical subjects of orthodox (Sunnī) Islām. It is also a summary of major earlier commentaries in Arabic. And it contains the teachings of Anṣāri himself. Arabic quotations in the text are sometimes translated into Darī-Persian. However, in many instances, Anṣāri (and later, Maybodī) seem to have overlooked the fact that the commentary is not in Arabic, with the result that many lines (and sometimes a few pages) are entirely in Arabic. Nevertheless, it is the only adequate source in Darī-Persian which elucidates the "ten schools of (Quranic) recitation" (qirā'āt al-'as͟hara) that is recognized as accurate among the earliest scholars of the Qur'an. We can also read in the "Kas͟hf al-Asrār" the Darī-Persian translations of each school of recitation (qirā'āt), following, a brief explanation of the morphological, syntactical, and stylistic aspects of the particular version of recitation.

Level 3: Ṣūfī (esoteric) commentary. This is an exposition of selected (not all) verses belonging to the section. The commentary here is mystical and includes sayings, poetry, and stories of the Ṣūfī masters.[3] Some analytical passages follow the style of the "Hundred Grounds" (Sad Maydān) and would be suitable as additions to the commentaries of the "Sad Maydān" (and of the "Manāzil") in a future publication.

The text of the "Kashf al-Asrār" is dotted with Anṣāri's axioms, exhortations, prescriptions, and aphorisms. Often, Maybodī makes it quite clear that he is providing a precise quotation of the words of the "Master of the Path" (Pīr-é Ṭarīqat). There are Arabic and Darī-Persian poems, some by Anṣāri himself. Some poems of Sanā'ī of Ghazna (d. 1131 C.E., or a few years later) seem to have been added to the text by Maybodī himself. Ecstatic words suddenly emerge in a didactic and scholarly treatise.[4]

All the "intimate invocations" (munājāt) which are in the text of "Kashf al-Asrār" were selected and published by Moḥammad Āsef Fekrat in Afghānistān.[5] This was also done during the same year by Dr. Jawād Sharī'at in Irān[6] The latter scholar also wrote "Fihrist-é Tafsīr-é Kashf al-Asrār,"[7] a remarkable index in Persian of this important work, which provides references to the ten volumes of the 1960 Tehrān edition.[8]

The "Kashf al-Asrār" has also been summarized in two volumes entitled "Tafsīr-é Khwāja Abdullāh Anṣāri," by Ḥabīb-ullāh Āmūzgār.[9] This summary, reprinted seven times, contains Levels 1 and 3 only of the commentary, and is therefore attractive to the lovers of Ṣūfī literature in Irān and Afghānistān.

Selections from "Commentary on the Qur'an" **(Kashf al-Asrār)**

The following is an analytical table of Anṣāri's commentary on a short chapter from the Qur'an, chosen as a literary specimen:

Table D

A Summary of the Contents of a Specimen from the "Commentary on the Qur'an" (Kashf al-Asrār) Chapter (Sūrah) 61, the "Battle Array" (Al-Ṣaff), revealed in Medīnah

Verse Number	Beginning word(s) of the verse	First Level Literal Trans. into Darī-Persian (Semantic examples)	Second Level Common (Exoteric) Commentary	Third Level Ṣūfī (Esoteric)
0	Bismillāh...	Raḥmān = ferākh bakhshāyesh	———	Spiritual value of Bismillāh
1	Sabbaḥa...	ba pākī = besotūd	Significance of praising God (text in Arabic)	Praise of God must be based on love.
2	Yā ayyuhā...	lima = che + rā	Importance of acts and action -Battles	Significance of sincerity
3	kabura...	maqt = zeshtī	Circumstances in which the text was revealed.	Commands of God to Jesus
4	inna 'Ilāha	bunyān = dīwār	Unity in battle	Jihād against innovations
5	wa idh qāla Mūsā...	zāghū= begashtand	People of Moses insulting him	———
6	wa idh qāla 'Īsā...	muṣaddiq = rāst dārenda	Jesus speaking of the coming of the Prophet of Islām	———
7	wa man...	iftarā = dorōgh mē-sāzad	Those saying falsehoods about God	———
8	yurīdūna...	kariha = doshwār āyad	They cannot extinguish the Light of God	———
9	huwa...	dīn al-Ḥaqq = kēsh-é dorost	The Truth of Islām shall prevail	———
10	yā ayyuhā...	tunjīkum = bāz rehānad	Meaning of tejārat (bargain)	Spiritual combat (jihād)
11	tu'minūna...	khayr = beh	Different ways of jihād	Wayfarers on the Path
12	yaghfir...	'adn = hamēshī	Description of Paradise reported by Abū-Hurayra	-Paradise -The Beverage of Purity in the Gathering of Intimacy

13	wa ukhrā...	naṣr = yārī	Meaning of "glad tidings" (text in Arabic)	———
14	yā ayyuhā...	ayyadnā = dast dādēm	Jesus' disciples' victory	———

The following is an example of Level 3 (nawbat al-thālitha) commentary translated from the original Darī-Persian:[10]

(About God)

The Establishment (istiwā) of God on the Throne ('Arsh) is in the Qur'an (20:5, 57:4). I have faith and belief (imān) in this. I do not seek any interpretation (ta'wīl) for it. This would be rebellion (ṭughyān). I agree with the evident (ẓāhir) meaning and also submit (taslīm) to the hidden (bāṭin) meaning (of the text).

Such is the creed of the Sunnis (the orthodox). Their way is to believe in the unseen (nā dar-yāfta) with (heart and) soul. My belief (imān) is based on the hearing (sam'ī); my Law (shar') is based on the related (khabar—text), and my knowing (ma'rifat) is what is found out (yāftanī). I am confirming (muṣaddiq) the related (text). I am the follower (muttabi') of what is heard (sam') through the instrument of the intellect (ālat-é 'aql), with the indication of revelation, with the message of the Messenger, and with the (required) condition (sharṭ) of submission (taslīm).

I know, however, that He is not "established" out of need (ḥājat). I know that the Throne is not "upholding" God, the Most Exalted. It is God who is the Owner (Dārenda) and the Maintainer (Negāh-dārenda) of the Throne. He has created the Throne for the seekers of God (Khodā-jōyān) and not for the knowers of God (Khodā-shenāsān). The knowers of God are different from the seekers of God. It is to the seekers of God that He said, "The Most Gracious is firmly established on the Throne" (Q. 20:5). He said to the knowers of God, "And He is with you" (Q. 57:4), by person (dhāt) on the Throne, by (His) knowledge ('ilm) everywhere, by companionship (ṣuḥba) in the spirit (jān), and by nearness in the soul (nafs).

* * *

O knightly man (jawān-mard)!
Do not dwell in the seclusion (khalwat) of "He is with you" (57:4),

Because "high above all is God, the King, the Truth" (20:114)
is also there.
Do not repose in "We are nearer than the jugular vein" (50:16),
Because "They do not make a just estimate of God" (6:91) is also
there.
Do not be bold in view of "Some faces will beam (in brightness)
that Day, looking toward their Lord" (75:22-23),
Because "No vision can grasp Him" (67:103) is also there.

Anything "He is the First" (57:3) offers,
Is taken away by "He is the Last (57:3).
Anything "He is the Evident" (57:3) gives,
Is made to fade away by "He is the Hidden" (57:3).

* * *

Why all this?
This is because:
The believer has to move between fear and hope; and:
The knower ('ārif) has to move between grasping (qabḍ)
and stretching (basṭ).

* * *

One cannot say:
"One cannot find (Him)"
This would be said by an antagonist.
One cannot say:
"One can find (Him)"
This would not be allowed by the Might ('Izzat — of God.)[10]

NOTES

1. Printed in ten volumes in Tehrān, 1960, by the late : 'Alī Asghar Ḥikmat. See Bibliography.
2. See G. Bowering, "The Quranic Commentary of al-Sulamī," in *Islamic Studies Presented to Charles Adams*, by W.B. Hallaq and Donald Little (Leiden: Brill, 1991), p. 49.
3. Anṣāri's commentary greatly influenced Ḥusayn Wā'iẓ Kāshifī, who incorporated selected texts of it into his Persian commentary on the Qur'an entitled "Mawāhib 'Aliyya" (completed in 899/1493-1494), generally known as "Tafsīr-é Ḥusaynī" and printed many times in India, Pākistān, and Irān.

4. This sudden change of subjects reminds us of the style found in certain chapters of the Qur'an, such as 55 (al-Ṭalāq), verses 2, 5, 7, 10-12.
5. Kābul, 1976.
6. Sokhanān-e Pīr-é Herāt, 1976.
7. Tehrān, 1984.
8. This edition was reprinted twice.
9. Iqbāl, Publ., 1970 in two volumes. This selection was later reprinted in one binding of 1253 pages.
10. "Kashf al-Asrār," Vol. 6, p. 114.

THE CONDEMNATION OF
SCHOLASTIC RATIONALISM

(DHAM AL-KALĀM)

BY 'ABDULLĀH ANṢĀRĪ OF HERĀT
(1006-1089 C.E.)

Selected texts translated from
the original Arabic

PRELIMINARY NOTES

"Kalām," literally, speech, logos, means "dialectic applied to Islamic theology." The first Islamic theologians were called Mu'tazilites, who in the second and third centuries (Hijra) insisted in applying reason to religious matters. The Jahmites (followers of Jahm ibn Ṣafwān, d. 128/745) thought that God has no attributes, because He is beyond comprehension. Abū-l-Ḥasan ibn Ismā'īl al-Asha'rī (d. 324/935) became a well-known figure among the "people of Kalām" (ahl-é kalām). The influence of his followers was resented, not only by the Sufis, but also by the Sunni scholars of Islamic jurisprudence, ritual, and law (fiqḥ).

"The Condemnation of Scholastic Rationalism and its People" (Dham al-Kalām wa Ahl-ihī) is a bulky manual in Arabic of anti-scholastic polemics.[1] Its date is not known. What we are presenting here shows Anṣārī's fundamental views on faith, creed, and Islamic scholarship. He quotes Quranic verses and a great number of Traditions of the Prophet (aḥādīth, accompanied by long chains of transmission —isnād) to show that the Jahmites, the Ash'arites, and all those who rely only on methods of rational philosophy in matters of creed of religion, have abandoned the ways and the spirit of Islām.

Serge de Beaurecueil, in his "Khwāja Abdullāh Anṣārī,"[2] has quoted a few selected pages of the "Condemnation," preceded by a table of contents (chapter titles) of the book. The table indicates that Anṣārī provided the material in order to demonstrate that, not only the Qur'an and Tradition (Sunnah) prohibit the rationalistic approach to religion (and therefore, the adherence to scholastic doctrines), but so did the great figures of Islām, such as Imām Shāfi'ī (d. 205/820).[3]

Selections from "The Condemnation of Scholastic Rationalism (Dham al-Kalām)

The most outstanding scholars of the Community and the most knowledgeable among the Sunnis (ahl al-sunnah)[4] have noticed that the scholasticism of the Jahmites[5] and all that they have borrowed from the teachings of Philosophers (falāsifa)[6] leads only to denial of the Divine Attributes. It was found that the center of their creed was the declarations of the atheists (zanādiqa) who preceded them, who said that: "The celestial sphere (falak) is turning and the Heavens are empty. God is everywhere and in everything, and He made no exception (in this regard) of the interior of a dog or a pig or the bowels (of people). God escapes (firār) all demonstration and all verification. God is the Hearer (Samī') without hearing (sam'), the Viewer (Baṣīr) without vision (baṣar), the Knower ('Alīm) without learning ('ilm), and the Mighty without might. God is the Divinity (ilāh) without soul (nafs), person (shakhṣ), or form (ṣūrat)." Then, they said: "He has no life (ḥayāt). He is not a thing (shay'), because if He were a thing, He would resemble things."

The Jahmites altered the teaching of the early leaders of the atheists when they declared: "The Creator (al-Bārī') is neither an attribute (ṣifat) nor a non-attribute (lā-ṣifat). They "feared" (in pretence) for the hearts of those Muslims who were weak (ḍa'f), who were heedless, or unable to discern.

Their apparent concern with the Qur'an was, in fact, avoiding and seeking protection from the sword. They pretended to act as followers of monotheism (tawḥīd) while engaged in dialogue with Muslims, and yet they were wearing priests' garments.[7] By their sayings, only their faults were shown; by their utterances, their bad faith became well-known; and by their outcries, the implications of their aphorisms became manifest. So much misfortune happened to them in their days from the sword of the Caliphs, from the opinions expressed by the learned religious scholars ('ulamā), and from their being abandoned by the masses.

I have filled my book, "The Impiety of the Jahmites" (Takfīr al-Jahmiyya) with the sayings of the learned scholars ('ulamā) of Islām, the sanctions of the Caliphs, and the attacks of the common people of the Sunnī[4] community against them, as well as the general agreement (ijmā') of the Muslims to excommunicate (i<u>kh</u>rāj) them from the Community (millat).

It is not hidden to intelligent people that the earlier and the later scholastic rationalism is like the same thread of women magicians (<u>kh</u>ayṭ al-saḥḥāra). Now, listen, O intelligent ones, to the changes (in the creeds) adopted by the later ones compared to the earlier ones: The earlier ones had said — may God make their words disgraceful! — that God is everywhere. The later ones say, "God is nowhere and no place can be attributed to Him." The Messenger of God, the peace and salutation of God be upon him, as quoted by Mu'āwiya b. al-Ḥakam, has said where God is. The adepts of scholastic rationalism, however, say, "He is as much above as below, and one cannot discover where He is. No place can be attributed to Him. He is not in the heavens and He is not on earth."" They deny direction and limit (ḥadd). The earlier ones said, "He has no speech; He created speech." The later ones say, "He spoke once and is speaking the same speech without interruption, and this speech cannot be found where He is not." Then they say, "He has no place." They say, "He has no voice (ṣawt) and no speech (ḥarf)." They say (about the Qur'an): "This is a cover and paper." "This is (made of) wool and wood." "The purpose of this (writing) was (to make) marks (naq<u>sh</u>)." "This was for breathing, which is the voice of the reader." "Do you imagine that anything good or bad may come from this, or that these are His words?" "Do you see (the professional reader) being payed for this?" One of their leaders said, "Since the Qur'an is in wool (labad)..." And then one said: "In wood." While maneuvering, they said, "This is a story (ḥikāyah) expressing what is in the Qur'an, and God spoke once and did not speak any further." And yet they said (to appear faithful), "The Qu'ran is not created, and the one who says it is created is unfaithful."

Such are the snares by which they want to capture the hearts of the common people of Sunnah.[4] In fact, the Jahmite males once, and the Ash'arite females, ten times, expressed their (real) creed, that, "The Qur'an cannot be found no-where (<u>gh</u>ayr mawjūd)." The Jahmites said, "No attributes!" The Ash'arites said (about some terms in the Qur'an): "(God's) 'visage' (wajh) has the same (symbolic) meaning as in (the Arabic expressions) 'the face of day,' 'the face of a matter,' 'the face of speech.'(God's) 'eye' ('ayn) has the same (symbolic) meaning as in (the expression) "the eye of enjoyment. (God's) 'hearing' (sam') has the same (symbolic) meaning as in the expression 'the wall's ear.' (God's) 'gaze' has the same (symbolic) meaning as in (the expression) 'the two walls gaze at each other." They said, "The 'Footstool' (kursī, of God, Q. 2:255) only means (Divine) 'Knowledge.' The 'Throne' ('arsh, of God, Q. 20:5) means (Divine) 'Kingdom.'" Then they said, "The person of the Messenger of God, peace be upon him, is not living. After his death, he was no more a conveyer of a message (muballigh), and there is no need to go for pilgrimage to his tomb..." You could not investigate any of their teachings without their (trying) to deceive you, or search into their beliefs without their (trying to) make you collapse into skepticism![8]

NOTES

1. Not yet published. Manuscripts are in the British Museum, 27520; Damascus, Om.24/587; Ankara University, 7614/1-2.
2. 1965, pp. 204-221.
3. See articles on "Allāh," "Kalām," "Jahmites," "Al-Ash'arī," in the *Encyclopedia of Islam,* New Edition, (Leiden, 1960 -).
4. The word "Sunnī," here, is not the opposite of "Shī'a" but the opposite of scholastic rationalists.
5. The followers of Jahm ibn Ṣafwān Abū-Muḥriẓ, d. 128/745.
6. 'Abdullāh Anṣārī views the "philosophers" (falāsifa) as distinct from the scholastic rationalists, but recognizes the impact of the former upon the latter.
7. Ṭaylasān — shawls or mantles worn by Christian priests.
8. Text translated from arabic, as quoted by S. de Beaurecueil, 1965, pp 204-221.

THE GENERATIONS OF THE ṢŪFĪS

(ṬABAQĀT AL-ṢŪFIYYAH)

BY 'ABDULLĀH ANṢĀRĪ OF HERĀT
(1006-1089 C.E.)

Selected texts translated from the original Darī-Persian

PRELIMINARY NOTES

It is clear that this work is not a "book" in the strict sense of the word. A study of this compilation of student notes indicates that:

1. In order to teach students and novices about past Ṣūfī masters, Anṣārī chose as a "textbook", the "Ṭabaqāt al-Ṣūfiyyah" by Abū-'Abdur-Raḥmān as-Sulamī (d. 1021 C.E.), which by that time was a recent and reliable Arabic manual in this field.[1]
2. While explaining the text in spoken Persian, Anṣārī provided significant additional information, reports and quotations — all noted by his students (see the following chart).
3. One, or possibly more, students presented his own compilation of notes in Persian in the form of a book, with very limited improvement in its form and began almost every paragraph with, "Shaykh 'Abdullāh Anṣārī said." As it stands, the work is more a compilation than a formal book. Some fragments of the compilation seem to have been added a few years after Anṣārī's death.
4. The compiler incorporated some of Anṣārī's sayings, "intimate invocations" (munājāt), and explanations of Ṣūfī subjects (see the following chart).

No systematic edition of the work has been done by the compiler. The older spoken Khorāsānī dialect was adopted as the most available basis for recording, while the text of "Kashf al-Asrār," "the Hundred Grounds" (Sad Maydān), and contemporary works (like the *History* of Bayhaqī) prove that literary Darī-Persian (the origin of "classical Persian") existed in those times as the accepted style for writing. The writing of notes in dialect form was not usual, and was something that Mawlānā Jāmī (d. 1492) complained about.[2]

The earlier (1961) Kabul edition[3] is no longer considered as an adequate source of study, since a new and improved edition

TABLE E
Chart of the Contents of
"The Generations of the Ṣūfīs" (Ṭabaqāt al-Ṣūfiyya)

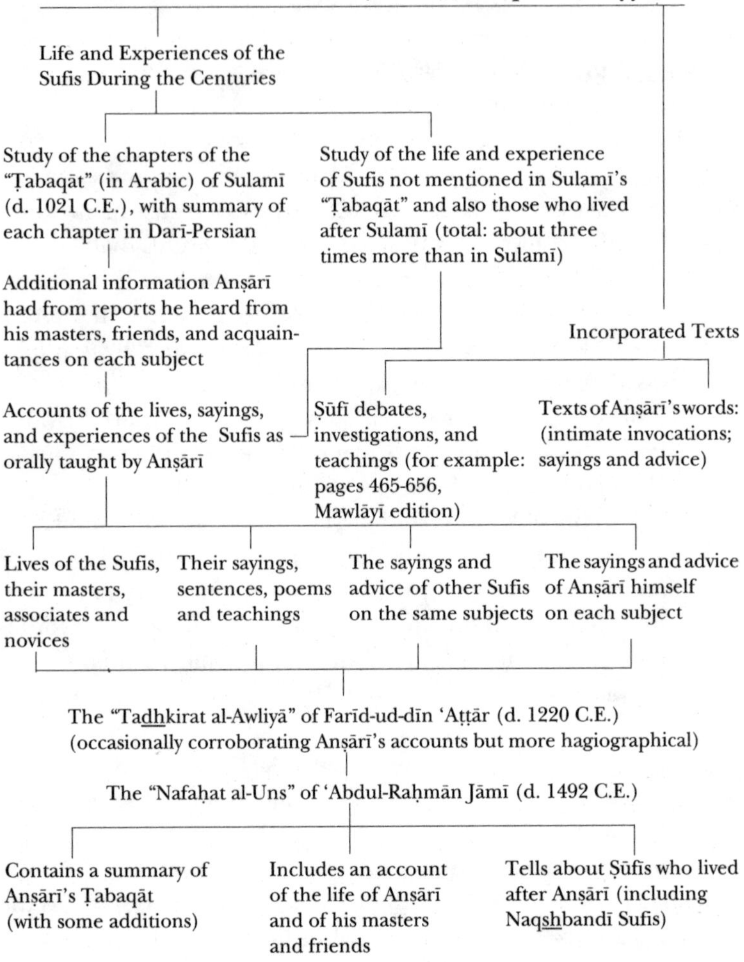
Life and Experiences of the Sufis During the Centuries
Study of the chapters of the "Ṭabaqāt" (in Arabic) of Sulamī (d. 1021 C.E.), with summary of each chapter in Darī-Persian
Study of the life and experience of Sufis not mentioned in Sulamī's "Ṭabaqāt" and also those who lived after Sulamī (total: about three times more than in Sulamī)
Additional information Anṣārī had from reports he heard from his masters, friends, and acquaintances on each subject
Incorporated Texts
Accounts of the lives, sayings, and experiences of the Sufis as orally taught by Anṣārī
Ṣūfī debates, investigations, and teachings (for example: pages 465-656, Mawlāyī edition)
Texts of Anṣārī's words: (intimate invocations; sayings and advice)
Lives of the Sufis, their masters, associates and novices
Their sayings, sentences, poems and teachings
The sayings and advice of other Sufis on the same subjects
The sayings and advice of Anṣārī himself on each subject
The "Tadhkirat al-Awliyā" of Farīd-ud-dīn 'Aṭṭār (d. 1220 C.E.) (occasionally corroborating Anṣārī's accounts but more hagiographical)
The "Nafaḥat al-Uns" of 'Abdul-Raḥmān Jāmī (d. 1492 C.E.)
Contains a summary of Anṣārī's Ṭabaqāt (with some additions)
Includes an account of the life of Anṣārī and of his masters and friends
Tells about Ṣūfīs who lived after Anṣārī (including Naqshbandī Sufis)

(1983) is available, made by Muḥammad Sarwar Mawlāyī[4] an Afghan scholar and resident of Tehrān. The Mawlāyī edition (of 968 pages), which contains notes, variants in the manuscripts, and indexes based on a few old manuscripts,[5] proves that no adequately edited text of the compilation has reached us. The 200 pages of indexes provided in the edition (especially the names of Sufis) are very useful to the researcher.

Selections from "The Generations of the Sufis" (Ṭabaqāt al-Ṣūfiyyah)

[THE BEGINNING OF THE TABAQĀT]:

In the name of God, the Most Gracious, the Most Merciful. Praise be to God, the praise He deserves! Blessing and salutations be to His messenger, the most purified of His creation, Muḥammad, peace be upon him, and to his kinfolk!

The Shaykh, the great Imām, the Shaykh al-Islām, the supporter of the Tradition (Sunnah — of the Prophet), the adornment of the learned religious scholars (al-'ulamā) is Abū-Ismā'īl, Abdullāh, b. Abī-Manṣūr Muḥammad, b. Abī-Mu'ād 'Alī, b. Muḥammad, b. Aḥmad, ibn 'Alī, b. Ja'far, b. Manṣūr, b. Abī-Manṣūr Mat al-Anṣārī, may God sanctify his soul and glorify his face. Mat Abū-Manṣūr came to Herāt with Aḥnaf b. Qays in the time of Uthman ibn 'Affān, may God be pleased with him, who is a descendent of Abū-Ayyūb Khālid b. Zayd al-Anṣārī al-Khazrajī al-Najjārī al-Azdī, the "Companion of the Saddle of the Messenger of God." peace be upon him. And the Messenger of God, may the blessings and salutations of God be upon him, stayed in his house in Medina during the time of his Emigration.

* * *

(Anṣārī) was asked, "What is the benefit to novices of these stories (of the shaykhs)?" He replied, "Allāh says, may His Name be glorified: 'And all that we relate to you (O Muḥammad) of the stories of the messengers, we make your heart firm with it: in them the Truth comes to you, as well as an exhortation, and a message of remembrance to those who believe' (Q. 11:120). (God says in this verse): 'If grief and anguish cause torment to you, O Muḥammad, you will hear about the earlier Prophets' stories and ponder on them. You will know that they proved to be firmly patient against grief and anguish. They trusted (in God) and relied on Him. By this, the resolve of your heart will be increased, and you will be able to persevere.' And God, the Most Glorious, says to him (Muḥammad): 'Therefore, patiently persevere, just as did (all) the Messengers, endowed with firmness, bore themselves with patience...' (Q. 46:35). And, "So wait with patience for the command of your Lord, and do not be like (Jonas) the companion of the Fish...' (Q. 68:48).

"In the same way, to learn the sayings of the righteous and the stories of the shaykhs (pīrān) and their (spiritual) states (aḥwāl) helps the edification (tarbiyyat) of the novice and increases his strength and resolve. With all that, he gains firmness against the trials and His probations. The novice will be steadfast on the path of poverty (darwēshī) and privation (nā-kāmī). This will permit him to gain the resolve of men (mardān) and to have recourse to the spiritual leaders, in order to learn from their behavior and character.

"Also, knowing the shaykhs and their friends will make you (O novice) related to them. Muṣṭafā,[6] peace be upon him, says, 'A person shall be together with the one who is dear to him.' (This means that) tomorrow (in the Hereafter) a person will be with the one to whom his heart is devoted today. God, the Most Exalted, says in his Firm Book: 'All who obey God and the Messenger are in the company of those on whom is the grace of God: the Prophets, the Sincere, the Martyrs, and the Righteous. Ah! How beautiful is their company!' (Q. 4:69).

"The least benefit from learning about the shaykhs is to notice that one's own deeds, (spiritual) states (aḥwāl) and sayings is not like theirs. (The novice) will then abandon selfishness (manī) from his behavior and will view his own flaws, to which he will compare the deeds of the shaykhs. The novice will free himself from arrogance, ostentation, and from considering himself as better than others, and will be humbly ashamed of (the defects of) his own deeds.

"When the novice learns and hears about the acts, sayings, (spiritual) states, behavior and character of (the shaykhs), he will knock at their doors to eagerly seek their company. In the days of (spiritual) indigence and destitution, they will be his benefactors. This is because friendship brings about (family) relationship (nisbat). It has been said (in Arabic) that 'the best of family relationships is friendship (al-mawadda),' and 'no (family) nearness of relationship is closer than friendship and no distance is greater than hostility ('adāwa).' "

* * *

"Abū-l-'Abbās ibn 'Aṭā (of Baghdād, d. 309/922) said: 'If you can't grasp His Friendship, grasp friendship with His friends. For friendship with the friends of God is (equivalent to) Friendship with God...'"

* * *

And the <u>Sh</u>ay<u>kh</u> al-Islām (Anṣārī), may God sanctify his soul, said to us (the student-novices): "From each spiritual leader (pīr) you have to remember a saying. If you do not recall their names, remember their sayings, and benefit from them. There is a blessing in listening (and learning) the words of the shaykhs. These words are agreeable to the heart. Your heart will incline toward those shaykhs..."[7]

[END OF THE TEXT TRANSLATED FROM THE BEGINNING OF THE TABAQāT.]

Abū-Hā<u>sh</u>im al-Ṣūfī (d. Circa 150/767)

I heard from the <u>Sh</u>ay<u>kh</u> al-Islām (Anṣārī), may God honor his face, that he said: "The first person to be called 'Ṣūfī' was Abū-Hā<u>sh</u>im al-Ṣūfī. He was a shaykh in Syria (<u>Sh</u>ām). His origin was from Kūfā. He lived in the times of Sufyān <u>Th</u>awrī. Sufyān <u>Th</u>awrī said, 'Were there not Abū-Hā<u>sh</u>im al-Ṣūfī, I would not know about Ṣufism'. Sufyān <u>Th</u>awrī died in Baṣra in the year 161 (778 C.E.), and also Ibrāhīm b. Adham, may God the Most Exalted have mercy on both of them!'

"And before him there were great Sufis. They had renounced worldly pleasures and were devoutly God-fearing, with eminent behavior, being on the path of trust in God (tawakkul) and the path of love (maḥabbat). But the name of 'Ṣūfī' was first said about him (Abū-Hā<u>sh</u>im).

"In ancient times, the Ṣūfī path (taṣawwuf) was more narrow and confined (tang) and was not wide (compared to today), since the times were delicate (nāzok). They (the Sufis) were more careful (ṣāyin) in their utterances. They strove hard in their (Ṣūfī) behavior (mu'āmalat), not in much speech and discourse, for they were calm and serene (mutamakkin). However, among the later generations (of Sufis), the guardianships (walāyat) became more apparent. Making speeches and declarations became more predominant. The Sufis were led to ecstasy, (spiritual) intoxication (sukr), agitation (qalaq), and excitement (<u>gh</u>alyān). They uttered in speech what they discovered (in their spiritual experiences). And this way became more evident in the second generation (of the Sufis)."

The <u>Sh</u>ay<u>kh</u> al-Islām said, "Manṣūr 'Ammār Dima<u>sh</u>qī said that, 'Abū-Hā<u>sh</u>im was sick and near death. I went to visit him. I asked, 'How do you feel?' He replied, 'I am finding it to be a great trial (balā'). But Love is stronger than trial.' He meant that the trial is great, yet small compared to Love (mehr)."

* * *

"Once Abū-Hās̲h̲im met S̲h̲uraik Nak̲h̲'ī coming out of the house of Yaḥyā K̲h̲ālid. He said (to him), 'I seek refuge in God from the knowledge that is not useful' (a'ūd̲h̲u bi-llāh min 'ilm-in lā yanfa').[7] The meaning of (this judgment was that he (Nak̲h̲'ī) was a judge (qāḍī — who was given his position on the basis of great learning). However, this story has also been attributed to others besides him (Abū-Hās̲h̲im).

"Abū-Hās̲h̲im has also said, 'To remove a mountain with a needle is easier than to throw off vanity and arrogance (kibr) from the heart.' S̲h̲ayk̲h̲ Sīrwānī has said, 'The last thing coming out from the hearts of the righteous is the love of (worldly) leadership (ḥubb al-riyāsat)."

The S̲h̲ayk̲h̲ al-Islām dictated to us that Muḥammad b. al-Junayad said, 'Being famous (s̲h̲uhra) is a temptation and a trial (fitna), and (yet) everyone is desirous of it. Not being famous is tranquility, and (yet) the one who is satisfied with it is rare.'" But this has been said before him (Muḥammad b. al-Junayd).

The S̲h̲ayk̲h̲ al-Islām, may God sanctify his soul, said, "In Dāmg̲h̲ān, S̲h̲ayk̲h̲ Abū-Ja'far, whose name was Muḥammad Qaṣṣāb Dāmg̲h̲ānī, a student of S̲h̲ayk̲h̲ Abū-l-'Abbās Āmolī, may God may have mercy on (both of) them, said to me that he heard from Abū-Muḥammad Tīnī the following: 'The first Ṣūfī convent (k̲h̲ānaqāh) was built in Ramallah, in Syria (S̲h̲ām). There was a Christian prince (amīr) who went on a hunting trip one day. On the way, he saw two men belonging to this group (ṭā'ifa — of the Sufis) come together, embrace each other, sit down, put what they had to eat in front (of each other), ate, and left. The Christian prince admired the friendship that he witnessed and asked one of them, "Who was he?" "I do not know." "What family relationship does he have with you?" "None." "Where is he from?" "I do not know." The prince said, "Then what is this friendship that is shared between you?" The dervish (Darwēs̲h̲) replied, "It is our Way." The Prince asked, "Do you have a place where you come together with each other?" He replied, "No." The Prince said, "(Then) I will build a place for you where you may come together. "And he built the khānaqāh in Ramallah.' "[8]

* * *

Abū-Sa'īd Aḥmad al-Kharrāz (d.277/890)

The Shaykh al-Islām (Anṣārī), may God sanctify his soul and make his light complete, said: "The name of Abū-Sa'īd Kharrāz is Aḥmad b. 'Īsā. He is a Baghdadian and leader (imām) in this path (of Sūfism). He is unique (yagāna), without equal. He is one of the most eminent of shaykhs. He has left many books and compositions. He was a student of Muḥammad Manṣūr Tūsī. He had acquaintance and companionship (ṣuḥbat) with Dhū-n-Nūn al-Miṣrī (d. 859 C.E.) and with Abū-'Abdullāh Nabbājī, Abū-'Ubayd Bisrī, Sarī Saqaṭī (d. 867 C.E.) and Bishr Ḥāfī (d. 841 C.E.), and (others) besides those. It has been said: he is the first one who spoke about the knowledge of subsisting (baqā) and annihilation (fanā)."

The Shaykh al-Islām said: "He (al-Kharrāz) represents himself as a student of Junayd (d. 910 C.E.), while, in fact, he was a patron (bār-khudā) of Junayd. He is one of the friends and peers (yārān wa aqrān) of Junayd. He was older (meh) than him (Junayd) and died before him in 277 (H), and God knows (best about those dates). He was originally from Baghdād, but during the afflictions (miḥnat) of the Sūfīs (there) he went to Egypt. For some time he was in Mecca. Murta 'ish says: 'When Kharrāz talks about realities, everything other people (say) is superfluous (wabāl)' ". The Shaykh al-Islām said, "In the knowledge of unification (tawḥīd), I knew no one superior to him (Kharrāz) from among the shaykhs. Everyone else compared to him is superfluous, including Wāsiṭī (d. after 932 C.E.) and Fāris 'Īsā Baghdādī."

It has been said that he is called "the piercer" (kharrāz) because he was piercing beads. He was asked, "Why do you continue to do this?" He replied, "I keep busy with this so that they won't make me busy (with something else)!"

The Shaykh al-Islām said, "If only Abū-Sa'īd Kharrāz were a little lame! Because no one was able to go with him (because of his speed in walking on the Ṣūfī path). If only Wāsiṭī had a little compassion (for his novices)! And if only Junayd were (spiritually) a bit sharper (tēz)! Because he was too scholarly ('ilmī)." And he said, "It is said that Ḥuṣrī (d. 981 C.E.) was the seal (khātim) of the knowers ('ārif—of God). This does not mean that he was the master (mawlā) of the seal of the knowers. And it is said that the chief (sayyid) of the knowers was Abū-Yazīd (Bisṭāmī—d. 874 C.E.). This does not mean that he was the master of the chief of the knowers. The sign (nishān) for humanity (ādamiyān) was Aḥmad the Arab (the Prophet Muḥammad), blessing and peace be upon Him! And the sign (nishān) for (Ṣūfī) wayfarers (rahiyān) was Abū-Sa'īd Kharrāz. The earth was filled with Kharrāz and could not contain him."

The Shaykh al-Islām said, "Kharrāz said, 'The beginning of this work (kār — Sufism) is being accepted (qabūl), and the end of it is finding (yāft).' And he said, "The Truth is not lost, so it must be sought for; and it is not distant, so it must be attained. The one who has found the Found-One (Mawjūd) is excused (ma'dhūr) by it. The finding, to us, is the discovering of the (spiritual) state (ḥāl) and the knowledge of the state without the (very) state itself (bi-lā ḥāl)." The Imām (Anṣārī) then said (in Arabic):

"The witnessing of finding (al-wujūd)
is the passing away (fawāt) of finding.
When all that is attained,
the purity of resolve (ṣafā' al-quṣūd) is gained."[9]

* * *

The Shaykh al-Islām said that, "Mardān Nahāwandī said that Abū-Sa'īd Kharrāz was asked, 'Who is the annihilated one (fānī)?' He replied, 'The one who abandons both his share of this world and the Hereafter and (does) not (abandon) God, the Most Exalted.'

"Abū-Sa'īd Kharrāz said: 'Unification (tawḥīd) has seven stages (maqāmāt):

'The first stage is gathering (jam') everything together (in the mind).

'The second stage is thinking (al-tafakkur) about everything.

'The third stage is collectedness in everything (al-jam' fī kulli shay').

'The fourth stage is annihilation (fanā') of everything.

'The fifth stage is setting up everything (iqāmatu kulli shay')

'The sixth stage is coming out (al-khurūj) from everything.

'The seventh stage is beginning with what is appearing in manifestation through it (badā' fī mā bihi tajallī), and appearing in manifestation with what is beginning through it (tajallī fī mā bi-hi badā').[10]

"Kharrāz said, 'The stages of the knowers (of God — ahl al-ma'rifat) are:

(1) Bewilderment coming from impoverishment (al-taḥayyur 'ani 'l-iftiqār); then (2) joy (surūr); then (3) annihilation with vigilance (al-fanā' ma'a 'l-intibāh); then (4) subsistence with watchfulness (al-baqā' ma'a 'l-intiẓār). And no created being attains (a degree) superior to this.' "

The Shaykh al-Islām said, "Kharrāz would have been (kāmastēd) a prophet because of his greatness. He is the leader (imām) of this affair (Sufism).

"He (Kharrāz) said, 'The ostentation of the knowers is better than the sincere affection (ikhlāṣ) of the novices.' He also said, 'To have patience (ṣabr) with (the trials sent by) God is the purpose of God in creating.' "

* * *

The Shaykh al-Islām said: "When Kharrāz was in (the plain of) 'Arafāt (near Mecca) and they (the pilgrims) were fervently praying the supplications (du'ā) of the Pilgrimage (Ḥajj), he said: 'A desire came to me, and I said (to myself) that I might also supplicate. (But) what supplication would I make? I resolved to make a supplication, in (all) sincerity (to God) that nothing (worldly) be left to me. (Then) a voice called to me and said, "After finding Me (wujūd-é Mā), still you are soliciting?" — meaning "You are wanting something after finding Me?" ' "

* * *

The Shaykh al-Islām said, "Abū-Bakr Kattānī (d. 934 C.E.) wrote a letter and sent it to Egypt to Abū-Sa'īd Kharraz: 'Since you left here, so much hostility has appeared among the Ṣūfis, and affection (ulfat) has vanished (from among them).' He wrote back his answer: 'This is the sanction of God against them, since they have no intimacy (mu'ānasat) between themselves."

* * *

The Shaykh al-Islām said... "When Kharrāz went to Egypt, during the afflictions of the Ṣūfis (in Baghdad), they asked him,

'Why do you not speak, O chief of the (Ṣūfī) folk?' 'These people,' he said, 'are absent (ghāyib) from God. To mention God to the absent is (like) backbiting (ghībat).' "

* * *

The Shaykh al-Islām (Anṣārī) said, Kharrāz was banished from Egypt. He was asked: 'What did they banish you for?' He replied, 'I said to them (that) there is no screen (ḥijāb) between me and God.' "[11]

[TRANSLATION OF TEXTS ABOUT LATER SUFIS]

Abū-l-'Abbās Qaṣṣāb Āmolī

His name (Shaykh Abū-'Abbās Qaṣṣāb) was Aḥmad b. Muḥammad b. 'Abd-al-Karīm. He was the Shaykh of Āmol and Ṭabarīstān, a follower of the school of Aḥmad (ibn Ḥanbal), a leader of this (Ṣūfī) work, a pure Hanbalite, a guide (qibla), and the chief (spiritual) Helper (ghawth) of his time. He said, "This business of our will go along with Kharaqānī." So he became close to Kharaqānī. He was told that Shaykh Sulamī had written (a book) on the generations (ṭabaqāt) of the (Ṣūfī) shaykhs. He asked, "Has he mentioned my name in it?" They said, "No." He replied, "Then he has done nothing!"

He was kind to the people of Herāt. Many of the shaykhs were like this, for they respected the Heratis. (And it is) right, since the Heratis are cordial (nēkō-del) people.

Shaykh Abū-l-'Abbās was talkative and was rarely silent. Otherwise, he was praying. He was a (spiritual) guide (qibla) in this work during his time.

He was (still living) in my time. Shaykh 'Amū (my teacher) was always saying to me,[12] "It is my wish to pay a visit to three mentors: Shaykh Abū-l-'Abbas Qaṣṣāb in Āmol, Shaykh Aḥmad Naṣr in Nishāpūr, and Shaykh Abū-l-'Alī in Merv." And he said to me, "I shall go there in the spring time (and) I will take you with me." Of course he never did take me (to Āmol) and it was not our lot and destiny. However, people used to keeping coming from near by it (Āmol) to the Ṣūfī convent (khānaqāh) of Shaykh 'Amū (in Herāt). I was always asking them about his (spiritual) states and sayings. No body knows about his states and sayings more than myself. He said, "Time (waqt — meaning the spiritual moment) is an alchemy."

* * *

The Shaykh al-Islām said, "If Kharaqānī and Muḥammad Qaṣṣāb were both to come back (to life), I would send you (novices) to Muḥammad (Qaṣṣāb), not to Kharaqānī, for he would be more useful to you than Kharaqānī "—meaning that Kharaqānī was one who has "finished" (muntahī—who had reached the final stages of the Ṣūfī path); a novice (murīd) would have learned little from him, unless he were a "finished one" (himself). And he (Qaṣṣāb) was better for novices.

* * *

The Shaykh al-Islām said, "In Jadāda, I heard about Shaykh Muḥammad Qaṣṣāb, that one day, Abū-'Abdullāh Ḥannāṭī came to speak with him. Ḥannātī was scholastic rationalist (mutakallim — a doctor of Kalām). Shaykh Abū-l-'Abbās said something (and) he rejected it. The shaykh stood silent. He did not speak that day and that evening, until dawn (when) he shouted, 'I am His servant in Islām. (The Prophet) Muḥammad is my protector (mawlā) in keeping the (Divine) Law (Shari'at). I adopted poverty (darvēshī); my claim is that I am nothing. Tell anybody who has this (spiritual condition) to come. Muṣṭafā (the Prophet) invites (people) to the (Divine) Law (Sharī'at), and I am inviting (people) to the (Divine) Reality (Ḥaqīqat).'" The Shaykh al-Islām explained: "He said that because Muṣṭafā is the reality (ḥaqīqat) in the Law, which is the pretext (bahāna) for (attaining) the Reality."[13]

Abū-Manṣūr al-Iṣfahānī

Abū-Manṣūr Mu'ammar b. Aḥmad al-Iṣfahānī was the Shaykkh of Iṣfahān, a descendent of the Prophet (sayyid), a leader (imām) in the knowledge of the outward (ẓāhir) and the knowledge of (spiritual) realities — unequalled among the shaykhs of his time, a Hanbalite, and a Sunnī."

The Shaykh al-Islām (Anṣārī) said, "No one has described the (spiritual) stages and stations (maqāmāt) better than him. Many (others) relate stories and anecdotes (ḥikāyāt) but the words of Sufis must be said on the basis of finding (wujūd), spiritual 'taste' (dhawq) and direct vision (didār) and not on the basis of anecdotes. Abū-Manṣūr had an eminent language. He is the author of books: 'The Path of the Elect' (Nahj al-Khāṣṣ), 'Forty (Traditions) for the Sufis'[14]

(Arba'īn) — an outstanding manual, and the book of 'Exile' (Ghurbat). In the book of 'Exile' he quotes a man who said: 'I found those who reached the farthest states (aṣḥāb al-ghāyāt) in these (Ṣūfī) matters (amr) who are withdrawn (ifrād — from worldly affairs).'

* * *

"Shaykh Aḥmad Kōfānī had met him, so I asked him if he remembered any of his words. He replied, 'No, but one day he was saying while talking, "The poor one is cherished" (al-faqīru 'azīz-un)'. I said (to Shaykh Aḥmad Kōfānī), 'One such phrase from a spiritual guide (pīr) is full and complete (tamām)' and he said, 'I wish that I had heard him explain (his book) "The path of the Elect," but he said, "That is very much entangled (jarr)" — meaning difficult. "And now, time is limited. I give you permission (to study the treatise)." ' "

The Shaykh al-Islām said, "Abū-Manṣūr Mu'ammar (al-Iṣfahānī) said: 'It is wrong to make comparisons (of common people) to the Prophets, because the common people are going toward temptation (fitna) while they (the Prophets) are (going) toward protection ('iṣmat — from sin).' "[15]

Sharīf Ḥamza 'Aqīylī

He was in Balkh. He was an ascetic and (a Ṣūfī) possessed of extraordinary acts of magnanimity (karāmāt). The father of the Shaykh al-Islām (Anṣārī) had years of companionship with him, and held him in the highest respect. Sharīf Hamza said, "I was in the Sacred Mosque the Masjid al-Harām, in Mecca) and I was performing two sections (rak'at) of the ritual prayer (namāz) in the 'Station of Abraham' (maqām Ibrāhīm — near the Ka'aba), when Khiḍr,[16] peace be upon him, appeared and said to me, 'Hamza! Get up and circumambulate (ṭawāf — around the Ka'aba) so that (your two sections of) ritual prayers can (also) be performed in Khurāsān!'" There are many anecdotes about his (Sharīf Ḥamza's) discernment and perspicacity (firāsat) and extraordinary acts of magnanimity (karāmāt).

The Shaykh al-Islām (Anṣārī) said, "My father (Abū-Manṣūr Anṣārī) served him (khidmat kard) for (long) years. When I was born in Hert, at the (very) same time he said in Balkh (to his companions), 'Our Abū-Manṣūr just had a son, and what a son!' "[17]

[ABOUT AN EARLIER SŪFI]
Ḥusain b. Manṣūr al-Ḥallāj

(d.309/922)

...Sheikhs do not agree on his case. Generally they reject (radd) him. Only three of them approve him: Ab-ul 'Abbās 'Atā, Abū-'Abdallāh Khafīf and Abu-l Qāsim Nasrābādī. Because of the Skeikhs, the Law (Shar') and the Knowledge ('ilm), I do not approve him but I do not reject him. Do the same (as I do)! Suspend (your judgment) on him. I like more those who approve him than those who reject him.

...Ibrāhīm Fātik, his disciple, the evening after Ḥallāj was executed, found the Presence of God in a dream and asked Him: "What you have done with Ḥusain, Your servant ?" God said: "I devlivered My Secret to him. I gave him a gift. He became arrogant (ra'nā), and convoked the people to himself, and disclosed the Secret to them!"

We translated only a few lines of this section. See: Ṭabaqāt, pp 381-390; Nafaḥāt of Jāmī, pp, 153-158.

NOTES

1. Edited by Nūr-ad-dīn Shuraybah, Cairo, 1953. Also edited by Johannes Pederson, Leiden, 1960.
2. In his preface of the "Nafaḥāt." See our Bibliography.
3. Edited by 'Abdul Ḥayy Ḥabībī, and reprinted afterwards in Tehrān.
4. An Afghan scholar residing in Tehrān. See Bibliography.
5. Dated 671 H./1271 C.E., 839/1434, 862/1457.
6. Muṣṭafā, "the Chosen," is a title of the Prophet Muḥammad.
7. An invocation said by the Prophet.
8. From pp. 1-8, Mawlāyī edition - See "Nafaḥāt" of Jāmī pp 27, 28.
9. From pp. 159-160, Mawlāyī edition.
10. The meaning of the seventh stage is that, after emerging from the state of annihilation, the Ṣūfī is in a renewed condition in which his actions are inspired by what originates within him in the state of unity, and in which appearance is in harmony with what emerges from the state of unity (without concealment or pretense).
11. From pp. 181-184, Mawlāyī edition.
12. Another manuscript has: 'I was always saying to Shaykh 'Amū..."
13. From pp. 372-75, Mawlāyī edition.
14. Meaning forty sayings (aḥādīth) of the Prophet that are especially loved by the Sufis.
15. From pp. 624-25, Mawlāyī edition. About "Path of the Elect", See page 59.
16. (Khiḍr (Pronounced "Khizr" in Persian) refers to Qur'an 18:65 "One of Our servants." Traditional narratives give this name (not mentioned in the Qur'an). He is a mysterious man who knows some secrets of the paradoxes of the Divine Will. He meets some righteous people without revealing his name to them. It is believed that he is immortal until the Day the last of the humans lives on Earth.
17. From page 157, Mawlāyī edition.

THE HUNDRED GROUNDS

(SAD MAYDĀN)

BY 'ABDULĀH ANṢĀRĪ OF HERĀT
(1006-1089 C.E.)

Selected texts translated from the original Darī-Persian

PRELIMINARY NOTES

The purpose of Abdullāh Anṣārī in originating this manual is clearly found in the text of his preface that we have translated here. The second title is "The Records of the Lectures On (the articles of) Faith" (Tarājem-è Majāles-è 'Aqīda). If we translate the word "tarājem" as "translation," this would suggest, incorrectly, that the "Hundred Grounds" was originally in Arabic and then rendered into Persian. Therefore, we are inclined to keep the meaning of (written) "records" and "exposition." The records seem to have been taken down by students because it seems that Anṣārī used to dictate his works as teaching materials. The dictation started on New Year's Day (Naw-Rōz), on March 21, 1056 C.E.[1] coinciding with the lunar New year day, 448 of Hijra.

The "Hundred Grounds" was the first didactic treatise on Sufism to be written in Darī-Persian and was specifically intended to serve as a *mnemonic* manual for novices to help them to remember teaching. This is why its memorization has been made easy through itemization and sub-itemization into ternary forms (3 + 3 + 3).

Anṣārī obviously followed the only mnemonic work in the field of Sufism, the "Path of the Elect" (Risālah Nahj al-Khāṣṣ) by Abū-Mansūr Isfahānī (d. 418/1207). This was written in Arabic, was structured into forty chapters (on Repentance, Devotion, Truthfulness, Sincerity, Self-examination, etc.), and featured three spiritual stations (maqām) in each chapter. Anṣārī venerated Abū-Mansūr Isfahānī highly and mentioned (in his "Generations of the Sufis") having read and admired this book.[1] In fact, in both of these works, we find that Abū-Manṣūr Isfāhanī and 'Abdullāh Anṣārī follow the style of the Traditions (ahādīth — sayings of the Prophet) in which the ternary structure 1 + 1 + 1) is often found.[2]

An English translation exists of the "Hundred Grounds," entitled "The Hundred Fields Between Man and God," translated by Dr. Munīr Aḥmad Mughal.[3] However, this translation suffers from many inaccuracies, generally caused by mistaken readings of the original Persian text.

While waiting for an accurate translation of the "Hundred Grounds," we offer here translations of some of its sections.

Numerous points concerning the "Hundred Grounds" and two other Arabic treatises of Anṣāri ("Stations of the Wayfarers" and "Flaws in the Stations") will be made in the introductions to both of these works.

TRANSLATION

***Selections from "The Hundred Grounds"* (Sad Maydān)**

In the Name of God, the Beneficent, the Merciful. Praise be to God, who shows to His protected ones (awliyā') His signs (āyāt), so that they will recognize them.[4] May His blessing be on the Sire of the Messengers, Muḥammad, and on all his kinfolk (ahl-ihī).

The Records of the Lectures on Faith

Words from Him: "Say (O Muhammad), 'If you love God, then follow me, (and) God will love you'" (Q. 3:31).

Beginning: the first of the month of Muharram, 448 (March 21, 1056 C.E.)

It has been reported that the Prophet Khidr, peace be upon him, said, "Between the servant and his Master, there are a thousand stages (maqām)." Similar (words) are reported from Dhū-l-Nūn Misrī, Bāyazīd Bistāmī, Junayd, and Abū-Bakr Kattānī, may God be well-pleased with all of them. Dhū-l-Nun said, "a thousand (road sign) banners (a'lām)." Bāyazīd and Junayd, may their secrets be sanctified, said, "a thousand cities (miṣr)." Abū-Bakr Kattānī said, "a thousand stages (maqām)."

God, the Most Exalted, said, "Is one who follows the pleasure of God like the one who has earned displeasure from God and whose abode is Hell? It is an evil destination! There are grades with God" (Q. 3:162-63). The grades (darajāt) that are (mentioned) in this verse are the thousand stages (maqām).

And there is the report (<u>kh</u>abar) from ('Umar) Fārūq-Allāh ibn <u>Kh</u>aṭṭāb, may God be well-pleased with him, confirmed by the entire community (ummah) with the chain of transmission cited in the two "Authentic Collections" (Ṣaḥīḥ, containing authentic Traditions, or sayings, of the Prophet),[5] that (the Archangel) Gabriel, upon whom be peace, asked the Messenger, may the blessings of God be upon him, "what is excellence (iḥsān)?" He answered, "That you worship God as if you see Him, because if you do not see Him, surely He sees you!"

The <u>Sh</u>ay<u>kh</u> of Islām (Anṣārī) said, "We have been informed by Muhammad b. 'Alī b. al-Ḥasan, by 'U<u>th</u>mān b. Sa'īd al-Dārimī, by Sulaymān b. Ḥarb, from Ḥammād b. Yazīd, from Matar al-Warrāq, from Abū-Burdah, from Yaḥyā (b. Ya'mur), from 'Abdullāh 'Umar, may God be well-pleased with them. With this chain of transmission, this saying is (authenticated and) completed. Muslim b. al-Hajjāj has given this chain of transmission in his "Authentic Collection" (Ṣaḥīḥ).

These thousand stages are stations (manzil-hā) through which the wayfarers are going toward God. The servant is either being transferred, grade by grade (daraja daraja), and he reaches the acceptance and proximity (qurb) of God the Most Exalted, or he himself proceeds station by station (manzil manzil) up to the last station,, the station which is for him the stage (maqām) of proximity (qurb). That proximity, to where he has travelled is for him a station (manzil); where he is held is a stage (maqām). This is like (the case of) the angels in the heavens (who say): "There is none of us but has an assigned place" (maqām — Q. 37:154), and, "They seek the means of access to their Lord, whoever of them will be nearest" (Q. 17:57).[6] Each of those thousand stages is a station to the wayfarer and stage to the dweller (pāyenda).

There are three (kinds of) men who speak about this knowledge:

First, the one who has realized (it — ahl-é taḥqīq);
second, the one who has heard (about it — ahl-é samā');
third, the one who claim (it — ahl-é da'wā).

(1) The realized one evidences illumination in his speech from "finding" (yāft),
(2) the one who has heard about it evidences alienation (bēgānagī) in his speech from "hearing," and
(3) the one who claims (to know it) evidences misery and ḍisgrace in his speech.

The affirmation of this knowledge is "finding" (it), and the sign of its soundness is its fulfillment (sar-anjām).

These thousand stages must not be cut off, for (even the time of) the twinkling of an eye, from six things:

(1) great respect for the (Divine) commandment (amr),
(2) fear of the (Divine) ruse (makr),
(3) necessity of apology ('udhr — to God),
(4) serving (God according to) the Tradition (Sunnah — of the Prophet),
(5) living in (spiritual) company (rifāqat), and
(6) kindness (shafaqat) toward people.

Since the Law (Sharī'at) is entirely the Reality (Haqīqat),
the Reality is entirely the Law,
the Law is the foundation of the Reality,
the Law without the Reality is useless,
and the Reality without the Law is useless,
those who act without these two are (themselves) useless.

The condition of each of these thousand stations is that you enter with the manifestation of repentance (tawba) and you exit with repentance. Because the Lord of Power said, "Turn in repentance to God, all of you, O believers!" (Q. 24:31).

He made all of His servants in need of repentance,
He revealed the baseness of sin for everyone, and
He afflicted everyone with the fault of heedlessness (ghaflat) and the inability to accomplish obligations.
Being without need (of anything from them),
He forgave (them) and
He was tender in exchange for (their) apologies.
For He said, "Whoever does not turn in repentance (toward God), those are the evil-doers" (Q. 49:11).
And He brought everyone created (into existence)
In accordance with (these) two determinations (those who will repent and those who will not).

The Chosen One (Muṣṭafā), may the blessings of God be upon him, made repentance the polisher of neediness and the excuse for deficiency, since he said, " I repent to You for all of my faults, and there is no power and no strength but in God,' 'the Exalted, the Supreme' (Q. 18:39 and 2:255)."

There are a thousand stages (maqām), from being acquainted
(ā<u>sh</u>nāyī — with Him) to having (His) friendship (dōstī).

And there are a thousand stations (manzil), from being aware (āgāhi
— of Him) to (having) bold familiarity (gostā<u>kh</u>ī — with
Him).

And all this has been established (néhāda) on a hundred grounds,
and God is the one whose help is asked!

1. REPENTANCE (TAWBA)

The First Ground is the stage of Repentance. Repentance is
returning to God. Words from Him, the Most Exalted: "Turn to God
in sincere repentance (tawba)" (Q. 66:8).

Know that:

knowledge is life,

wisdom is a mirror,

contentment (<u>kh</u>orsandī) is a fortress,

hope is intercession,

recollection (<u>dh</u>ikr — of God) is a medicine (for all ills), and

repentance is an antidote (taryāq).

Repentance is:

the signpost of the Way (né<u>sh</u>ān-é rāh),

the cargo master (sālār-é bār — of the caravan),[7]

the key to treasure, the intercessor for union,

the major mediator,

the condition for acceptance, and

the secret of all happiness.

The basic principle of repentance are three:

regret (pe<u>sh</u>aymānī) in the heart,

apology ('u<u>dh</u>r) on the tongue, (and),

severance from wickedness and wrong-doers.

The types of repentance are three:

the repentance of the obedient (muṭī'),

the repentance of the disobedient ('āṣī) and

the repentance of the knower ('ārif).

I. The repentance of the obedient is from overestimating (his
own) obedience and devotion (ṭā'at),

II. The repentance of the disobedient (sinner) is from
understimating (his own) insubordination, and

III. The repentance of the knower is from being oblivious of (God's) favours.

(1) Overestimating one's obedience and devotion has three signs:
first, considering one's self worthy of salvation through one's own acts (of devotion);
second, viewing those who are deficient with disdain; and
third, failing to seek for the flaws of one's acts (of devotion).

(2) Understimating one's own insubordination has three signs:
first, considering one's self worthy of (God's) forgiveness;
second, being untroubled by what is (spiritually) harmful; and
third, keeping company with evil persons.

(3) Being oblivious of (God's) favours has three signs:
first, ceasing to hold one's (selfish) self in contempt;
second, placing (too much) value on one's own (spiritual) state; and
third, not striving for the joy of friendship (āshnāyī—with God).

2. COMPASSION (MURU'A)

The Second Ground is Compassion. The Ground of Compassion emanates from the (First) Ground of Repentance (Tawba). Compassion is being humble and living restrained in one's self. Words from Him, the Most Exalted: "Be maintainers of justice and equity" (Q. 4:135).

The elements of compassion are three:
(living) intelligently (ba-'aql) with one's self,
living patiently (ba-ṣabr) with people, and
(living) needfully (ba-néyāz) toward God.

1. living intelligently with one's self has three signs:
knowing one's own value (qadr),
seeing the measure (andāza) of one's own performance (kār), and
striving for the betterment of one's self.

2. Living patiently with people has three signs:
being satisfied with them according to their abilities,
being lenient toward their excuses, and

giving them justice for their demands according to the (extent of) one's ability.

3. Living needfully toward God has three signs:
   (recognizing) gratitude (shukr) as mandatory (wājib) for anything coming from God,
   recognizing apology ('udhr) as mandatory for anything one is doing for the sake of God, and
   recognizing the Will (ikhtiyār) of God as right.[9]

* * *

(ground 3 to 67 not translated)

68. EXILE (GHURBAT)

The Sixty-Eighth Ground is Exile. The Ground of Exile emanates from the (Sixty-Seventh) Ground of Favour (Futūḥ).

Words of God, the Most Exalted: "...those possessing a remnant (of wisdom) in order to forbid (men) from corruption on earth..." (Q. 11:116).

Those "possessing a remnant (of wisdom)": are those (who are) exiled and expatriated (ghurabā'). Who are those exiled ones? May the Favour (of God) be upon them!

All the exiled ones are of three groups:

The first group are those excluded from their homes.
When living, they are guests;
when dead, they are martyrs; and
in the Hereafter, they are intercessors.

The second group are the believers (living) among hypocrites.
When living, they are combatants (mujāhidīn);
when dead, they are martyrs; and
in the Hereafter, they are intercessors.

The third group are the knowers ('ārifān — of God, living) among the heedless.
In the body, they are on earth;
in the heart, they are in the heavens; and
to the world and the worldly, they are strangers.

* * *

69. UNIFICATION (TAWḤID)

The Sixty-Ninth Ground is Unification. The Ground of Unification arises from the (Sixty-Eighth) Ground of Exile (Ghurbat).

Unification is:
to call One,
to see One, and
to know One.

Words of God, the Most Exalted: "Know, therefore, that there is no God but God" (Q. 47:19).

I. To call Him One:

This is the beginning of all knowledge,
the gateway to all worldly and religious knowledge, (and)
the partition between friend and foe. And

the profession of faith (in Divine Oneness and Unity) is the banner,
sincerity (ikhlās) is the foundation,
and faithfulness (wafā) is its precondition.

The Profession (of Unity) has three outward and inward aspects:

(1) To bear witness that God, the Most Exalted, is Uniquely One by His Essence (Dhāt) and is exempt from association with any spouse, progeny, rival, or associate — may His Purity be glorified and may He be Exalted!

(2) To bear witness that God, the Most Exalted, is Uniquely One in (His) Attributes (Ṣifat-hā) that are (His) beyond doubt. they (the Attributes) are beyond our reason. Their "how" is beyond perception, beyond containment and limit (of thought), and beyond imagination. In these (Attributes), He has no associate and He has no likeness — may His Purity be glorified and exalted!

(3) To bear witness that God, the Most Exalted, is One in His pre-eternal Names.

These Names are reality in regard to Him; to others are something borrowed.

Those (creatures) created by Him also have names, (but), His Names are, in regard to Him, properly Real, pre-eternal, (and) worthy of Him — while the names of created beings are created, contingent (muḥdath), (and) suitable to them.

"Allāh" and "Raḥmān" are His Names (only); by these Names no other being may be addressed (Q. 17:110).

II. To view Him as One

in (His) decrees (aqrār),
in (His) allotments (aqsām), (and)
in (His) bounties ('ālā')

(1) To view Him as One in His decrees (means that)
He is One in assigning providences (qadar-hā),
He is One in His infinite pre-eternal Knowledge ('ilm),
(and He is One) in (His) all-embracing pre-eternal Wisdom.
No one has the knowledge and the wisdom to realize this except Him:

the vision of this is the fruit of wisdom (ḥikmat),
the realization of this is the fruit of wonderment (ḥayrat), (and)
the furtherance of this is the fruit of power (qudrat).
None possesses that power except Him!

(2) To view Him as One in His allotments (means that) His bonuses to the creation are given out each by themselves: according to the proper share, known as good for all, (and) provided at the appropriate time (waqt).

(3) To view Him as One in His bounties (means that) He is by Uniqueness, the Giver (Mu'ṭī):
no one is deserving of gratitude and acknowledgment (minnat) except Him.
no one has (true) power (ḥawl) and might (quwwat) except Him, (and)
no one possesses the wherewithal to withhold (man') or to dispense (manḥat) bounty except Him.

III. To know Him as One

in serving (khidmat — Him),
in behaving (well) in one's (spiritual) actions (mu'āmalat),
in aspiring (himmat — to Him).

(1) Serving (Him) is
to renounce leadership (riyāsat — over others),
to observe sincere truthfulness (ikhlās), (and)
to control (one's own) thoughts (ḍabṭ-é khāṭir).

(2) Behaving (in one's spiritual) actions (is)
to purify one's innermost consciousness (sirr),
to realize the recollection (dhikr — of God), and
to steadfastly maintain one's confidence (i'timād — in God's Grace).

(3) Aspiring (is)
to lose sight (gom kardan) of everything except Him,
to forget everything except Him, (and)
to gain deliverance (bāz rastan) through the emancipation (āzādī) of the heart from everything except Him.

* * *

[grounds 70 to 95 not translated]

96. BEDAZZLEMENT (DAHSHAT)

The Ninety-Sixth Ground is Bedazzlement. The Ground of Bedazzlement arises from the (Ninety-Fifth) Ground of Intimacy ('Uns).

Bedazzlement is to be freed and separated from one's self during the assault of intimacy ('uns).

Bedazzlement is such a state
where the body is unable to maintain endurance (ṣabr),
where the heart is unable to care about the intellect ('aql), (and)
where the sight is unable to distinguish (between any thing).

(1) The body is unable to maintain endurance
when it is without the heart's deliverance (ferāghat-é del),
when awe (haybat) is separating one's body from one's heart, (and)
when the power of forbearance (ṭāqat) is weakened.

(2) The heart is unable to care about the intellect
when the spirit (rūḥ) is calling it
when the spirit is giving it ecstatic finding (wajd), (and)
when thirst (tashnagī) prevails.

(3) The sight is unable to distinguish (between anything)
when it is downed in the light of contemplation (mushāhada),
when the call of grace (luṭf) reaches it, (and)

when the veil of breathing (tanassum) is removed from it.

* * *

97.CONTEMPLATION(MUSHĀHADA)

The Ninety-Seventh Ground is Contemplation. The Ground of Contemplation arises from the (Ninety-Sixth) Ground of Bedazzlement (Dahshat).

Words of God, the Most Exalted: "...surely in that is a reminder for him who gives ear and is a witness (shahīd)" (Q. 50:37).

Contemplation is the removal of obstacles ('awāyiq) between the devotee and God.

The way (ṭarīq) it is threefold:

realization of the degree of wisdom (ḥikmat) by means of the degree of knowledge ('ilm);
attainment of the degree of purity (ṣafāwat) by means of the degree of patience (ṣabr); (and)
realization of the degree of reality (ḥaqīqat) through the degree of knowing (ma'rifat).

(1) Man attains the degree of wisdom by means of the degree of knowledge in three ways:
putting one's knowledge ('ilm) to good use,
venerating (God's) commandments (amr), and
adhering faithfully to the Traditions (Sunnah — of the Prophet).
And this is the stage of the sages (ḥakīmān).

(2) Man attains the degree of purity through the degree of patience in three ways:
abandoning contention (munāqashat),
renouncing (worldly) schemes (tadbīr), (and)
considering contentment (riḍā) as necessary.
And this is the stage of the one (who is) contented (rāḍī—with God's Will).

(3) Man attains the degree of reality through the degree of knowing in three ways:
reverence (toward God) in solitude (khalwat),
reproaching one's self for inadequacy in rendering due service (to God), (and)
preferring (īthār) one's companions above one's self.

* * *

98. (DIRECT) OBSERVATION (MU'ĀYANA)

The Ninety Eighth Ground is (Direct) Observation. The Ground of Observation emanates from the (Ninety-Seventh) Ground of Contemplation (Mushāhada).

Words of God, the Most Exalted: "Have you not looked to your Lord, how He has spread out the shadow?" (Q. 25:45).

Observation is seeing total perfection.

And it has three aspects:

to regard Love with the eye of sympathetic compilance (ijābat),

to regard the Unique (Fard) with the eye of isolation (infirād), (and)

to regard the Ever-Present One (Ḥāḍir) with the eye of attending consciousness (ḥuḍūr).

I. The exposition of the first entails three things:

(1) to respond affirmatively to the (Divine) summons (nidā') through making humble entreaties and excuses ('udhr) by begging for it, (and)
to respond affirmatively to the (Divine) summons of Grace (luṭf) by soliciting it;

(2) to respond affirmatively to the (Divine) summons in making firms one's resolve (qaṣd) by concluding it, (and)

(3) to respond affirmatively to the summons of inner consciousness (sirr) by soliciting it;

II. The exposition of the second aspect means that:

(1) He is Unique in Guidance,
(so) keep on witnessing (shahādat — for) the Unique;

(2) He is Unique is Knowledge,
(so) continue expressing gratitude (shukr) to the Unique;

(3) He is Unique is Protection,
(so) keep the intent (irādāt—of devotion) to the Unique.

III. The explanation of the last aspect (is by means of)

(1) distancing from your "self,"
(so) be near His Nearness;

(2) being absent from your "self,"
(so) be present in His Presence;

(3) (knowing that) He is not far from those who resolve (qāṣidān — to reach to Him),
He is not missing to those who seek (ṭālibān — Him), (and)
He is not absent to those who (are) devoutly pursuing (murīdan — Him).

* * *

99. ANNIHILATION (FANĀ)

The Ninety-Ninth Ground is Annihilation. The Ground of Annihilation emanates from the (Ninety Eighth) Ground of (Direct) Observation (Mu'āyana).

Words of God, the Most Exalted: "All things perish except His Face. His is the judgment and to Him you will be returned" (Q. 28:88).

Annihilation is:
annihilation of the seeking in the Found,
annihilation of the knowing in the Known,
annihilation of the seeing in the Seen.
How can "that-which-is-nothing" ever find anything about "That-Which-Eternally-Is"?
(How can) Reality, which is eternally subsistent, ever be aligned with what is perishable?
(And how can) the unworthy be bound to the Worthy (Sazā)?
All, except Him, are of three categories:
the non-existent of yesterday,
the lost of today, and
the not-being of tomorrow.
Therefore,
all except Him are non-existent (nēst);
however, (they are) existing by (means of) Him (hast ba-Way),
so all existence is His (hama hast-é Way-ast).
The rain drop reached the sea and found therein its mellowing,
Just as the star was effaced by the daylight.

Whoever reached his Lord and Master (Mawlā) has attained his true "self."

* * *

100. SUBSISTENCE (BAQĀ)

The Hundredth Ground is the Ground of Subsistence (Baqā). The Ground of Subsistence emanates from the (Ninety-Ninth)

Ground of Annihilation (Fanā).

Words of God, the Most Exalted: "God is the Best, and the Everlasting (abqā)" (Q. 20:73).

God, the Most Exalted, is, and nothing else.

(For in this state)

attachments ('alāyiq) are severed,
secondary causes (asbāb) are destroyed, (and)
conventions and norms (rusūm) are nullified.

Limits (ḥudūd) are shattered,
understandings (fuhūm) are wrecked, (and)
histories (tārīkh) are obliterated.

Signs (īshārāt) are extinct,
allusions ('ibārāt) are effaced, (and)
expressions (khabar) are negated.

And God, the One and Unique, abides by Himself, eternally Subsistent!

Now

these Hundred Grounds
are all absorbed (mustaghraq)
in the *Ground of Love* (Maḥabba)!

The Ground of Friendship (Dōstī) is the Ground of Love.

Words of God, the Most Exalted: "...a people He loves and who love Him..." (Q. 5:54). "Say: 'If you love (tuḥibbūn) God...'" (Q. 3:31).

And Love has three stages:

first of all, uprightness (rāstī);
at midway, drunkenness (mastī); and,
finally, annihilation (nēstī).

And praise be to God, the First and the Last![9]

NOTES

1. See S.L. de Beaurecueil's edition of this Arabic treatise in "Mélanges Ṭāhā Ḥusayn," Cairo, 1962).
2. See the article of the author "The Hundred Grounds of 'Abdullāh Anṣārī of Herāt; the Earliest Mnemonic Ṣūfī Manual in Persian" in *Classical Persian Sufism*, edited by Dr. Leonard Lewisohn, London, 1993 (see Bibliography).
3. Islamic Book Foundation, Lahore, 1983.
4. This is based on Q. 27:93.
5. Refers to the famous collections of Traditions (aḥādīth) of al-Bukhārī and Muslim.
6. Or: "...(even) those who are nearest..."
7. This may also be translated as "master of the audience (with a king)" or "chamberlain."
8. From pp. 15-19 of Tehrān edition, which is based on the Cairo edition.
9. This is the end of the entire text (from the Cairo edition).

THE BOOK OF THE STATIONS OF THE WAYFARERS

(KITĀB MANĀZIL AL-SĀYIRĪN)

BY 'ABDULLĀH ANṢĀRĪ OF HERĀT
(1006-1089 C.E.)

Selected texts translated from the original Arabic

PRELIMINARY NOTES

If there is a classical Ṣūfī treatise with a clear structure, it is this work. Dictated in Arabic by Anṣārī who, by then, was blind, it contains:

1. A preface and an introduction
2. Ten sections (abwāb). Each section contains ten chapters, and each chapter presents a "station" (manzil).
3. An epilogue, which is at the end of the Hundredth Station of Unification.

The "Stations of the Wayfarers" was composed in 475/1082, twenty-five years after "Hundred Grounds" (Sad Maydān). The comparison of the orders of the spiritual stations in the "Stations" to those in the "Hundred Grounds" indicates the evolution of Anṣārī's views at the end of his career, seven years before his death. All the stations are aimed at attaining union (tawḥīd). For example, the Ground of Love, the last one in the "Hundred Grounds." is only the Sixty-First Station in the "Stations."

As we said in the case of the "Hundred Grounds," the main purpose of Anṣārī in the "Stations" was also to teach students and novices. The treatise, similarly, has the typical characteristics of an "aide-mémoire" with chapters, sections, and further divisions and subdivisions. To make learning by heart easier, the main division of the text as a whole is decimal (10 x 10), while the ternary (1 + 1 + 1) and the sub-ternary (3 + 3 + 3) systems are used in each chapter.

By adopting the mnemonic 10 x 10 = 100 division of the text together with the ternary system in the chapters and sections, Anṣārī made the memorizing of the text easier. On the other hand, and as a result of this system, there is an apparent "artificial" shaping of treatise. A study of his other Ṣūfī works ("Kashf al-Asrār," "Ṭabaqāt," and "Munājāt), however, indirectly demonstrates to us that the external format of the "Hundred Grounds" and the "Stations" was intended only to assist the memory of students, rather than to be artificially divided or simplistic.

The relentless mnemonic system also has another impact on our assessment of both treatises: the rigidity of the expositions. This rigidity certainly was a remedy for many trends existing among the common people and Ṣūfīs who were semi-literate, such as: (1) forgetting that spiritual travellers proceed toward Unity from one degree to another, and that the journey is marked by powerful and striking moments; (2) failing to recognize some stages and stations on the Ṣūfī path; (3) believing in an order of attainment of stages which is not corroborated by the experiences of the great masters of Ṣūfism.

The "Stations," like the "Hundred Grounds," should not be viewed as a manual of excessive theorization. 'Abdullāh Anṣārī had a vast knowledge of life and experiences of the great Ṣūfīs who preceded him, and he would never have put forth a system of principles contrary to their experiences.

The comparison of the "Stations" with the "Hundred Grounds" (as well as the Ṣūfī materials in the "Kashf al-Asrār" and the "Ṭabaqāt") make it clear that Anṣārī was aware of the diversity of spiritual experiences, especially of the striking and vivid impact of God's Grace on His chosen ones.

Serge de Beaurecueil, who spent long years studying the "Stations,"[1] rightly warned his readers not to be dupes of the apparently rigid structure of the "Stations," since spiritual experiences cannot be regimented. And one of the commentators on the "Stations," Shams al-Dīn Tabādaganī (end of the 9th/15th century), expressed the view that each of the stations has the characteristics of all the others. From another perspective, the descriptions of the consecutive stations, independent of their order, have a surprisingly "contemporary" quality.

Despite being so concise and succint, the "Stations" is not epigrammatic, crypitc, or overly laconic. It answers hundreds of questions asked by novices. And, as a treatise, it has no equivalent in earlier or later Ṣūfī literature. As Serge de Beaurecueil noted in "Chemin de Dieu," "Precision and conciseness join systematization with a purpose which is as much pedagogical as mnemotechnical."[2]

While the "Hundred Grounds" was read only in Persian in Khorāsān, the "Stations" was read in Arabic throughout the entire Islamic world of Anṣārī's time, from Khorāsān to Andalusia, and during subsequent centuries as well. The large number of commentaries on the "Stations" in Arabic and Persian is the best testimony of its distinction, as well as its notoriety.[3]

Selections from "Stations of the Wayfarers" (Manāzil al-Sāyirīn)

[THE BEGINNING OF THE BOOK]

In the name of God, the Beneficent, the Merciful.
Praise be to God,
the One, the Sustainer, the Stable, the Subtle, and the Near,
Who has poured upon the hearts of the knowers ('ārifīn) the rain of the most noble of words from the mist of wisdom;
who has beamed upon them the splendors of pre-existence (al-qidam) on the pages of non-existence ('adam);
Who has guided them to the nearest of the ways (aqrab al-subul) toward the first path (minhāj al-awwal);
Who has brought them back from the dispersion (tafarruq) (because) of deficiencies towards pre-eternity (azal); and
Who has scattered upon them from His treasuries (dhakhā'ir) and had entrusted them with his secrets (sarā'ir).
There is no divinity except God,
the One Who has no associate,
the First, the Last, the Outward, and the Inward (Q.57:3),
Who has spread the shadow of changes (talwīn) extended on the creation then made the sun of stability (tamkīn) a guide toward Him for the chosen ones,
and then withdrew the shadow of diversity (tafriqa) toward Himself in an easy withdrawal.[4]
And may His bountiful blessing and peace be upon His Chosen one, Muḥammad,
who has sworn to Him to establish His Truth, and upon his family!

***

[Preface]

A group of those desiring to learn about the stations of the wayfarers toward God, from among the Ṣūfis (fuqarā')[5] of the people of Herāt and those from other lands (g͟hurabā'), have been asking me to compose for them an exposition of the knowledge of these stations, to be a sign on their guideposts.

I have responded to them by this (manual) after begging for the guidance (istik͟hāra) of God and for His support.

They asked me to give an account of the stations: indicating (their) order to succession (tawālī), showing (their) divisions and branches (furū') —without quotations from anyone else, so as to be agreeable for recitation and easy for memorization.

* * *

[Introduction]

I was afraid of following, in this exposition, the words of Abū-Bakr al-Kattānī (d. 322/934), who said: "There are a thousand stages of light and darkness between the servant and God." I would then have produced (something) too long for myself and for them! Therefore, I have mentioned the foundations of the stages by pointing them out and indicating their goals.

I wish them (those asking me for this manual) to succeed, in accordance with the sincerity of their intentions. Abū -'Ubayd al-Busrī (d. 245/859) said, "God has such servants to whom He may reveal in their early stages what (would otherwise be) discovered (only) in their last stages."

I have assigned independent chapters and sections for the (stages) in order to avoid lengthy (texts) causing boredom (malāl) and (in order) not to leave questions unanswered.

I have therefore, prepared it in a hundred stages, (with) the total divided into ten parts.

* * *

Junayd (d. 297/910) said: "The servant is transported from one state (hāl) to a higher one, while a remnant of it is left to him from the state from where he was transported. By keeping that state from the (impact of) the earlier state, he may validate it (fa yuṣalliḥu-hā)." To me, a servant has no valid stage (maqām) until he rises up above it, dominates it, and then validates it (fa yuṣaḥḥihu-hū).

Know that the wayfarers through these stages are very different from each other, not agreeing on a specific order, and not standing on a common goal.

A number of early and late (authors) have composed works in this field. You may not find (all or) many of these works to be adequate or beneficial (to you), in spite of their qualities: Some indicate principles without providing details; some compile narratives (ḥikāyāt) without summarizing principles and without emphasizing axioms and precepts (nukta); some do not distinguish between the stages of those who are privileged (khāṣṣa) and the needs of commoners ('āmma); some count the ecstatic words (shaṭḥ) of the senseless (maghlūb) as a stage; some count the expressions of the (ecstatic) finder (wājid) and the allusions of the (already) established one (mutamakkin) as belonging to commoners; the majority do not talk about grades (darajāt).

Know that the majority of the scholars of this community (ṭā'ifa) and who point to this path agree that the last stages (nihāyāt) cannot be confirmed without authentically securing the early stages (bidāyāt), in the same way that a building cannot stand except upon a foundation.

The authentic securing of the early stages is (by):

(1) establishing the work of viewing with sincerity (ikhlaṣ),
(2) following the Tradition (Sunnah — of the Prophet),
(3) observing the interdictions by viewing with fear and observing with respect (ḥurmah),
(4) being compassionate toward humanity by offering advice and by not being a burden, (and)
(5) avoiding any company that might spoil the (spiritual) "moment" (waqt) and any condition that might put the heart into temptation (yuftin)

In this matter there are three kinds of people:

(1) The one (who is) engaged between fear (khawf) and hope (rijā), aimed toward love (ḥubb), and observing modesty and reserve (ḥayā). That one is called "murād."

(2) The one who has escaped the valley of dispersion (tafarruq) to the valley of concentration (jam' — on God).

(3) The one other than these two, (who) is only a pretender and a claimer and who is tempted (maftūn) and tricked (makhdu').

All these stages have three degrees (rutab):

The first degree is the starting of the journey by the one who is proceeding (qāṣid).

The second degree is entering into exile (ghurba).

The third degree is arriving at contemplation (mushāhada), which attracts toward essential unification ('ayn tawhīd) through the way of annihilation (fanā).

[Traditions/Aḥādīth]

(According to) the chain of transmission given that goes up to (Abū-Hurayra), the Messenger of God, may the blessing and peace of God be upon him, said, "Advance (sīrū)! (For) the singular ones (mufarridūn) will reach first."

They said, "O Messenger of God, who are the singular ones?"

He replied, "The quakers (muhtizzūn) who are quaking with the recollection (dhikr) of God, the Most Exalted. The recollection (of God) will free them from their (heavy) burdens (athqāl) and they will come with light burdens (of sin) on the Day of Resurrection."

This Tradition (ḥadīth) is "good" (hasan — in terms of authenticity).[6]

This Tradition is included in the "Collection" (Ṣaḥīḥ) of Muslim (also as), "The singular one will reach first" (sabaqa l-mufarridūn).

As to the meaning of entering into exile (ghurba):[7] Ḥamza b. Muḥammad b. 'Abdullāh al-Ḥusaynī informed us, from Abū-l-Qāsim 'Abd-al-Wāḥid b. Aḥmad al-Hāshim the Ṣūfī from Abū-'Abdallāh 'Allān b. Zayd al-Dīnawarī the Ṣūfī in Baṣra, from Ja'far al-Khuldī the Ṣūfī, from Junayd, from Sarī (Saqaṭī), from Ma'rūf al-Karkhī, from Ja'far b. Muḥammad, from his father, from his grandfather, from (Caliph) 'Alī, may God be pleased with him, who said that the Messenger of God, may the blessings and peace of God be upon him, said: "The search for God is (in) being exiled" (ṭalabu l-Ḥaqqi ghurbat-un).

This Tradition is rare (gharīb) and I have written it only on the basis of the (one) transmission of 'Allān. It is a Tradition concerning the attainment of contemplation (ḥuṣūl 'al al-mushāhada).

From (the report of) 'Ūmar b. al-Khaṭṭāb,[8] in the Tradition of the question (of) Gabriel (to) the Messenger of God, may the blessings and peace of God be upon him, he (the Archangel) asked, "What is excellence (iḥsān)?"

He (Muḥammad) replied, "That you worship God as if you see Him, for if you do not see Him, He certainly sees you!"

This Tradition is (also) rare. Muslim has given it in (his) "Authentic Collection" (Ṣaḥīḥ).

This Tradition is a general indication of the way (madhab) followed by this community (of the Sufis). I will explain to you the grades (darajāt) of its stages (maqāmāt) so that you may know

(1) the grade of the commoner ('āmma),
(2) then the grade of the one who is proceeding (sālik),
(3) and then the grade of the one who is realizing (muḥaqqiq).

For each one there is a way, a traced-out path,[9] and a goal toward which the turns.[10] A post has been planted for him to which he is appointed. (And) a final purpose has been assigned for him toward which he is prompted.

To fulfill this aspiration (qaṣd — for this manual), I am asking God that I may be accompained (by Him) and not isolated (from His Guidance).

Know that the ten sections about which I have talked in the beginning of this book are the following:

1. Beginnings (bidāyāt)
2. Doors (abwāb)
3. Actions (mu'amalāt)
4. Virtues (akhlāq)
5. Principles (uṣūl)
6. Valleys (awdiya)
7. (Spiritual) states (aḥwāl)
8. Guardianships (wilāyāt)
9. Realities (ḥaqā'iq)
10. Fulfillments (nihāyāt)

The Section of the Beginning has ten chapters:

1. Awakening (yaqẓah)
2. Repentance (tawba)
3. Appraisal (muḥasaba)
4. Turning (inābat — to Him)
5. Reflection (tafakkur)
6. Recollecting (tadhakkur)
7. Holding fast (i'tiṣām)
8. Escape (farār)
9. Austerity (riyāḍah)
10. Listening (samā')

1. AWAKENING (YAQẒAH)

God, the Most Exalted, says, "Say (to them, O Muḥammad): 'I exhort you to one thing, that you rise up (taqūmū) for God'" (Q.34:46).

To rise up (qawma) for God is:

to wake up from the slumber (sinat) of heedlessness (g͟haflat) and

to spring up (nuhūḍ) from the entanglement (warṭa) of lassitude (fatra):

it is the primary (source) from which the heart of the servant acquires the illumination of living by seeing the light of awakening (tanbīh).

Awakening has three aspects:

(I) Awakening through the heart's glance (laḥẓ) at the favours (ni'mah — of God),
by feeling hopeless in counting (all of) them, by understanding (the impossibility) of limiting their boundaries, by devoting oneself to the obligation (minnat — to God) for them, (and) by recognizing one's shortcomings in paying dues (ḥaqq) for them.

(II) Awakening through observing (his own) misdeeds (jināyāt), by understanding their dangers, by devoting oneself to putting them right, by freeing oneself from their snares, (and) by seeking salvation in rectifying (tamḥīṣ) them.

(III) Awakening through being aware of what is being gained or lost during the day,
by freeing oneself from losing (the gains), by caring about withholding them, by preparing oneself to make up in case of losing them, (and) by holding on to what persists of them.

(I) Knowing the favours of God is refined by three things:
(1) the light of the intellect (nūr al-'aql);
(2) watching the lightning of (Divine) Grace;
(3) keeping respect for those (who are) in trial (ahl al-balā').

(II) Observing of (one's own) misdeeds is correctly (implemented) by three things:
(1) knowing the magnitude of God (ta'ẓim al-Ḥaqq);
(2) knowing (one's own) self (nafs);

(3) believing in the threat (wa'īd — of God).

(III) And being aware of what is gained and lost is divided in three:

(1) listening to (Divine) knowledge ('ilm);

(2) responding to the call to be respectful (ḥurmah);

(3) keeping company with the righteous (ṣāliḥīn).

The prerequisite (milāk) for these is to rid (oneself) of (bad) habits ('ādāt).[11]

* * *

[STATIONS 2 TO 95 NOT TRANSLATED]

96. FINDING (WUJŪD)

God, the Most Exalted, has clearly used the name of "finding" (wujūd) in the Qur'an in the (following) places: He says, "...he will find (yajid) God (to be) Forgiving, Merciful" (Q. 4:110); "...they would have found (wajadū) God (to be) Forgiving, Merciful" (Q.4:64); "...and he finds (wajada) God" (Q.24:39).

Finding indicates conquering (ẓafar) the signification of the reality of something.

It has three meanings:

First, the finding of knowledge emanating from the Presence (ladunī — of God); it cuts off the knowledge of observation ('ulūm al-<u>sh</u>awāhid) by the soundness (ṣiḥat) of the disclosure (mukā<u>sh</u>afa) from God to you.

Second, the finding of God (by) the finding itself ('ayn al-wujūd); it cuts off any potentiality of indication (i<u>sh</u>āra).

Third, the finding of the state (maqām); (it causes) the vanishing (iḍmiḥlāl) of the (very) mode of finding (rasm al-wujūd) from submersion (istig<u>h</u>rāq) in the Primordiality (awwalīyyah)

* * *

97. CASTING ASIDE (TAJRĪD)

God, the Most Exalted, says (to Moses): "Put off your shoes" (Q.20:12).

Casting aside is the throwing off (in<u>kh</u>ilā') of the observation of testimonies (<u>sh</u>awāhid).

It has three grades (darajāt):

The first grade is casting aside discovery (ka<u>sh</u>f) itself and gaining the acquisition of certitude (yaqīn).

The second grade is casting aside concentration (jam‘) itself and reaching the attainment of (intuitive spiritual) knowledge (‘ilm).

The third grade is casting aside deliverance (khalāṣ — of oneself) and the observation (shuhūd) of casting aside (itself).

98. SEVERANCE (TAFRĪD)

God, the Most Exalted, says: "...and they will know that God is the evident Truth" (Q.24:25).

Severance means deliverance (takhlīṣ) from (the limitations of) allusions (ishārāt) to God (ilā l-Ḥaqq), by God (bi l-Ḥaqq), (and) from God (‘ani 'l-Ḥaqq).

I. Severance of (mere) allusions to God (is by)
   (1) purifying the intention (qaṣd) by means of thirst (‘aṭshan); then
   (2) purifying love (maḥabba) by consuming (talafan — oneself); then
   (3) purifying (temporary) contemplation (shuhūd) by (making it) continuous (ittiṣālan).

II. Severance of allusions by God (is by)
   (1) cutting off allusions due to pride (iftikhār) in denouncing (būḥan — it);
   (2) cutting off allusions belonging to conduct (sulūk) by studying it (muṭāla‘atan)
   (3) cutting off allusions due to seizing (qabḍ), by being jealous (ghayratan — about it).

III. Severance of allusions from God (is by)
   (1) expanding (inbisāṭ) in a manifest (way);
   (2) including pure seizing (qabḍ — by God);
   (3) guiding toward God and calling (others to Him).

99. CONCENTRATION (JAM‘)

God, the Most Exalted, said: "...and you (Muḥammad) did not throw when you threw, but it was God threw" (Q. 8:17).

Concentration casts away dispersion (tafriqa) and cuts off allusions (ishāra);
it distinguishes (man) from (being only) water and clay after the achievement of (its) stability (tamkīn);
it gives freedom from changing (talwīn),

deliverance from considering dualism (<u>th</u>anawīyya),
rescue from the feeling of flaws (i'tilāl), and
release from noticing its testimonies (<u>sh</u>uhūd).

Concentration has *three grades:*
the concentration of learning ('ilm), then
the concentration of finding (wujūd), and then
the concentration of concentration.

(1) The conentration of learning is the dispersion (talā<u>sh</u>ī) of the knowledge of contemplation in the knowledge emanating from the Presence (laduni — of God.)

(2) The concentration of finding is the dispersion of the achievement of continuity (ittiṣal — of the finding) in the essence of finding (itself which is) realized (muḥiqqan).

(3) The concentration of the essence (jam 'al-'ayn) of concentration is the dispersion of everything called allusion (i<u>sh</u>ārat) in the Essence (<u>Dh</u>āt) of God, in actuality (ḥaqqan).

Concentration is the ultimate aim (g<u>h</u>āya) of the wayfarer's stages. It is the shore of the Ocean of Unity (baḥr al-tawḥīd).

100. UNIFICATION (TAWḤĪD)

God, the Most Exalted, says: "God witnesses that there is no divinity except Him" (Q.3:18).

Unification is recognizing God as being free from being contingent (tanzīh 'ani 'l-ḥada<u>th</u>).

(Therefore), what the scholars ('ulamā') have spoken about (and) what the seekers of truth (muḥaqqiqūn) have indicated have all been (spoken and) indicated for correctly (teaching about) unification. Any other (spiritual) state (ḥāl) or stage (maqām) is accompanied by flaws ('ilal).

Unification has three aspects:

The first aspect is the unification of the commoners ('āmma), the authenticity of which is founded on testimonies (<u>sh</u>awāhid).

The second aspect is the unification of the privileged ones (<u>kh</u>āṣṣa), the support of which is upon realities (ḥaqā'iq).

The third aspect is the unification of the privileged among the privileged ones (<u>kh</u>āṣṣat al-<u>kh</u>āṣṣa), the support of which is preexistence (qidam).

I. *The first* (aspect of) unification is the attestation (shahāda) that there is no divinity except God (lā ilāha ill-Allāh), the One with no associates, "the Stable, Who begets not and is not begotten and there is none comparable to Him" (Q.112:2-4).

This is the main and manifest unification,

(for by it), the major associating of partners (shirk al-a 'ẓam — to God) is forbidden;

by it, the direction of prayer (qiblah) has been defined; (and)

by it, (religious) duty has become obligatory.

And by it, blood is spared and possessions protected;

by it, the Land of Islām is distinguished from the Land of Disbelief;

by it, belonging to the (religious) Community is approved for commoners.

And (in regard to commoners), even if (they) do not assert the correct declaration, they will be freed from uncertainty, perplexity, and doubt by (their) sincerity in the profession (of faith), authenticated through confirmation in the heart.

And this is the unification of the commoners fulfilled by testimonies (shawāhid), the testimonies being the mission (risāla — of the Messenger of God) and the works (ṣanā'i — of God). It becomes necessary (yujib) after hearing; it is discovered by viewing the Truth (tabṣīr al-Ḥaqq); it grows by attesting the testimonies (mushāhadat al-shawāhid).

II. *The second* (aspect of) unification, which is confirmed by Realities (ḥaqā'iq), is the unification of the privileged.

It is the casting away (isqāṭ) of apparent causes (asbāb), going beyond intellectualistic debates, and going beyond dependence on testimonies (shawāhid).

In this (stage) you will not depend on any argument (dalīl) for unification, (you will) not (need any) cause (sabab) for trust (tawakkul) in God, and (you will) not (need any) means (wasīla) for salvation (najāt).

You will view the precedence (sabaq) of God in His Wisdom and in His Knowledge. (Everything will be seen) in how things are put in their place, in how things are relative (ta'līq) to their moments, (and) in how things are concealed (ikhfā) under their patterns (rusūm).

(By that way) you will realize the (knowledge of) causes ('ilal —and) you will step on the path of casting away (isqāṭ—the viewing of) new occurrences (ḥada<u>th</u>).

This is the unification of the privileged, which is achieved by knowing annihilation (fanā), (which) becomes clear by knowing concentration (jam' — on God), and attracts those (who enjoy) concentration to (reach) unification.

III. *The third* (aspect of) unification is the unification that God has specified for Himself and has (ordained) as being right to His Measure (qadar); (He) has projected (alāḥa) a beam (lā'iḥ) of it upon the inner secrets (asrār) of a number of His sincere friends (ṣifwat-ihi), made them mute so they won't describe (na'at) it, (and) rendered them powerless so they won't divulge it.

And the allusion made to this in the language of those alluding (is expressed through) the casting away (isqāṭ) of new occurrences (ḥada<u>th</u>) and the confirmation of pre-existence.

This (way of expression by) allegory (ramz), in this (aspect of) unification, is (itself) a fault ('illat). Unification will not be achieved unless this (fault) is cast away (isqāṭ).

This is the pole (quṭb) of allusions in the language of the masters of this (Ṣūfī) way (ṭarīq). They have furnished it with ornaments (zu<u>kh</u>ruf) of descriptions (and) they detailed it in chapters; while obvious explanations ('ibāra) only increase its hidden (<u>kh</u>afā) — character), descriptions (ṣifat) only increase its reticence (nufūr), (and) detailing (basṭ) only increases its difficulty (ṣu'ūbat).

Those who are engaged in asceticism (riyāḍa — and) those possessed of (spiritual) states (aḥwāl) are proceeding toward this (aspect of) unification.

Those who are revering (ahl al-ta'ẓīm — God) are intending (to proceed) toward it.

Those who are speaking on the essence of concentration ('ayn al-jam') are referring to it. Concerning it, allusion (i<u>sh</u>ārat) loses ground, tongues cannot speak, (and) expression cannot give (any) indication.

Because unification is beyond what any created one could

indicate about it, what time could encompass, (and) what any cause (sabab) could cover.

* * *

In former times I answered, in three couplets, a question asked of me by an inquirer about unification as viewed by the Ṣūfīs:

> No one can declare the Unity of the Unique:
> If anyone declares the Unity of Him, (he is) a denier!
>
> The declaration of Unity by anyone speaking from his own description
> Is something shameful and nullified by the Unique!
>
> The declaring of His Unity is for Him to declare!
> And the description of anyone describing Him is heretical!

> Mā waḥḥada al-wāḥida min Wāḥid,
> Idh kullu man waḥḥada-Hū jāḥid.
>
> Tawḥīdu man yanṭiqu ʻan naʻtihī,
> ʻĀriyat-un abṭala-hā ʻl-Wāḥid.
>
> Tawḥidu-Hu iyyā-Hu tawḥidu-Hū
> Wa naʻtu man yanʻatu-Hū lāḥid[12]

NOTES

1. He prepared and published the critical edition of this work in Arabic, translated it into French, and published some of the commentaries on it in separate books.
2. p. 39
3. See the list of commentaries in Beaurecueil's "Chemin de Dieu," pp. 47-55.
4. This is a paraphrase of Q.25:45-46.
5. Literally "poor ones." The singular of this Arabic word is "faqīr," referring to one who is nonattached to worldly matters and who cultivates "spiritual poverty." It was translated into Persian as "darwēsh" (poor one, or beggar) — spelled in the West as "dervish."
6. Here, Anṣārī gives three chains of transmission, two of which go up to Abū-Hurayra (as the one who heard the Prophet make the utterance).
7. Mentioned above as the second degree of three stages.
8. Just prior to this sentence, Anṣārī gives the chain of transmission for this Tradition going up to ʻŪmar (the Caliph).
9. This is a paraphrase of Q. 5:48.

10. This is a paraphrase of Q.2:148.
11. Here ends the first part of the manual (the preface, introduction, and first chapter), and here ends the selection from the beginning of the "Stations."
12. Here ends the selections from the "Section of Fulfillments" Chapters 96-100, plus the epilogue in poetry at the end of the manual.

THE FLAWS IN THE STATES

('ILAL AL-MAQĀMĀT)

BY 'ABDULLĀH ANṢĀRĪ OF HERĀT
(1006-1089 C.E.)

*Selected texts translated from
the original Arabic*

PRELIMINARY NOTES

This Arabic treatise, listed as Anṣārī's work by his earliest biographers, has a limited circulation (perhaps because of being so brief) and manuscripts of it are very rare.

This very concise work was dictated by Anṣārī a short time before his death to a young disciple, 'Abdul-Mālik of Karrokh (462/1071 - 548/1154).[1]

The word "'ilal" (the plural of 'illat) means deficiencies. The main purpose of this minor work is to warn novices about the spiritual risks in the stages of proceeding toward God. Anṣārī teaches that all of the ten spiritual stages, except unification (tawḥīd), have flaws and weaknesses that may lead seekers into various dangers.

S.L. de Beaurecueil has mentioned the impact of the "Flaws in the Stages" on the "Beauties of the Meetings" (Maḥāsin al-Majālis) written by the Andalusian Ṣūfī, Ibn al-'Arīf (481/1088 - 536/1141).[2]

Selections from
"THE FLAWS IN THE STAGES"
('Ilal al-Maqāmāt)

In the name of God, the Beneficent, the Merciful.

Shaykh Burhān-al-Dīn Abū-l-Fatḥ Yūsuf b. Muḥammad b. Muqallid al-Tanūkhī al-Dimashqī, may God be merciful to him, said: I have read to the righteous Imām, Shaykh Abū-l-Fatḥ, 'Abd-al-Mālik b. Abū-l-Qāsim al-Kharrokhī what I copied from his book, and he approved its accuracy. I read (that) the Shaykh al-Islām, Abū-Ismā'il 'Abdullāh b. Muḥammad al-Anṣārī, said:

This is the mentioning of some flaws that occur in the stages and which remain from the attention of the novice (murīd) who is a beginner (mubtadī).

* * *

1. WILL(IRĀDAH)

I. The will is (the focus) of the commoners ('āmma): it is carrying out aspiration (qaṣd—and) confirming the intention (nīyyat); (it is) resolution in the searching (ṭalab).

II. In the way of the one who is privileged (khāṣṣa), it is a disposition and a coming back to his own self (nafs). The will of (God's) servant is his very wish (ḥaẓẓ); this is the starting (point) for pretension (da'wā).

III. (The stages of) concentration, finding, annihilation are to be decided upon for the servant by his Master (Mawlā — God), (for) the One Who Wills is his Master:
"And if He wills good for you, there is none who can repel His bounty" (Q.10:107).

* * *

2. RENUNCIATION (ZUHD)

I. Renunciation is (the focus) of the commoners ('āmma): it is depriving the (carnal) self (nafs) of pleasures and denying it what is superfluous; (it is) shutting down frenzy and finishing off passion (hawā).

II. In the way of the privileged, mentioning "something without meaning" (mā lā-ya'nī) refers to this lowly world (and) desisting from exalting or appreciating it.

III. The principle of renunciation is to chastise the outward (ẓāhir) by abandoning this world, while staying concerned about being attentive to the inward (bāṭin). To remain interested in the world would be to return to your (carnal) self: you would fail to struggle against your "self" and against your (spiritual) moment (waqt) becoming spoiled, because of attending only to your own sensations. And you would stay permanently with yourself.
"...so give freely or withhold, without reckoning" (Q.38:39).

* * *

[SECTIONS 3 TO 9 ARE NOT TRANSLATED]

10. LONGING (SHAWQ)

I. Longing is the recollection of what is desired and the agitation of the "endurance" (ṣabr) of being deprived of it. This is for the commoners.

II. In the way of the privileged, it is a flaw, because longing is for the absent, while the One for Whom longing occurs is Present.

III. The Book (the Qur'an) and the authentic Tradition (Sunnah) do not mention "longing" (shawq) because longing speaks about "remoteness," makes allusion to "absence," and looks to "reaching," (while) "...He is with you wherever you may be" (Q.57:4)

* * *

11. THE WAY OF THE PRIVILEGED (ṬARĪQ AL-KHĀṢṢA)[3]

Know that nothing can be done, with (all) the means available in the creation, to reply to disciples seeking guidance (and answers for) very difficult questions (such as about) the "making of a hole in the ship of the destitute" and "the killing of the adolescent."[4] However, (what can be said is):

1. The will (irāda) of the privileged is to desist from all wishes (murādāt) by seeing in it (only) what God wants, for Him and only Him:
   "If He wills some mercy for me, can they withhold His mercy?" (Q.39:38).
2. The renunciation (zuhd) of the privileged is to keep (their) aspirations (himmat) away from the dispersion of the existent (world), because God has exonerated them from depending on circumstances, thanks to the Light of the Unveiling (nūr al-kashf):
   "We have purified them by means of a pure thought: remembrance of the Abode (in the Hereafter)" (Q.38:46).
3. The trust (tawakkul — in God) of the privileged is their contentment (riḍā) with the planning (tadbīr) of God and their freedom from their own (personal) planning, and their freedom from the anxious inclination to hand over their affairs to (themselves) to be taken care of. This is because of their expectation that the Planner (Mudabbir) is taking care of their affairs and is carrying them through on the basis of His knowledge of their interests (maṣāliḥ), as well as their freedom from engaging themselves in a controversy (munāza'a) with Him in the matter, (since they are)

"...well-pleased and well-pleasing" (to Him —Q.89:28).

4. The endurance (ṣabr) of the privileged is forbidding their hearts (to engage in) evil suspicion (khawāṭir — and) knowing that God has no decree (that is) deprived of compassion (ra'fat — or is) beyond clemency (raḥmat):
"He tests the believers by a fair test from Him" (Q.8:17).
5. The sorrow (ḥuzn) of the privileged is to lose all hope for (the part of) themselves which "commands to evil" (ammārat bi' ssū'—Q.12:53):
"Truly, man is ungrateful to his Lord." (Q.100:6).
6. The fear (khawf) of the privileged is awe and veneration (haybat) towards His Majesty (Jalāl — and) not fearing (His) chastisement ('adhāb). Because fearing chastisement is to strive for the self (nafs) in order to protect it, (while) awe and veneration toward (His) Majesty is to glorify God and to forget the self (nafs):
"They fear their Lord high above them" (Q.16:50).
7. The hope (rijā) of the privileged is their craving thirst (ẓama') for the beverage in which they are drowned and by which they are made drunk:
"Have you not looked toward Your Lord...?" (Q.25:45).
8. The thankfulness (shukr) of the privileged is their delight (surūr) with what they have found (bi mawjūd-ihim):
"Rejoice, then, in the bargain that you have made!" (Q. 9:111).
9. The love (maḥabbat) of the privileged is their annihilation (fanā) in the Love of God for His intimates (aḥibbā'-ihī):
10. The longing (shawq) of the privileged is their escaping from their own habits (rasm) and marks (simāt):
"I hastened to You, my Lord, that You might be well-pleased!" (Q.20:84).

All these stations — will, renunciation, trust, endurance, sorrow, fear, hope, thankfulness, love, and longing are stations of the people of the Law (Shar' — who are) journeying toward Reality (ḥaqīqah). But when they contemplate Reality, the stages (aḥwāl) of the journeyers will vanish,

so that what was not (always) there (mā lam yakun) will be annihilated, so that what was (always) there will subsist, and

so that what (always) was not (mā lam yakun) will vanish (yafnā):

"And the Fact of Your Lord will remain! (yabqā — Q.55:27).[5]

NOTES

1. This disciple was referred to earlier in our "Outline" of Anṣārī's life". Karrokh is a small town near Herāt, not to be mistaken with Karkh of Baghdād.
2. In Beaurecueil's "Chemin de Dieu," p. 77.
3. This section is a concluding summary.
4. Refers to Q. 18:60-82.
5. Here the treatise ends.

SAYINGS AND ADVICE

(MAQŪLĀT-O ANDARZ-HĀ)

BY 'ABDULLĀH ANṢĀRĪ OF HERĀT
(1006-1089 C.E.)

Selected texts translated from the original Darī-Persian

PRELIMINARY NOTES

These sayings of 'Abdullāh Anṣārī are incorporated in the different parts of the "Commentary on the Quran" (Kashf al-Asrār) and the "Generations" (Tabaqāt). We have selected these texts and have given it the title of "Sayings and Advice." These are, however, other maxims and advice of Anṣārī in later manuscripts.[1] The sayings and prescriptions of Anṣārī that are from the early manuscripts have been extracted and published by Dr. Jawād Sharī 'at, but not as an independent collection. It is not distinct from the "Intimate Invocations" (Munājāt). It is the rhetorical resemblance of the "Sayings and Advice" with the "Intimate Invocations" that has led to the publication of such a mélange.

A complete collection of these Darī-Persian sayings of Anṣārī based on the early manuscripts ("Kashf al-Asrār" and the "Tabaqāt") still needs to be prepared, edited, and published. Translations into other languages could then be made.

The "sayings and advice" of Anṣārī are in rhymed prose similar to his "intimate invocations". Some of these sayings are incorporated in the texts of the "Invocations." Titles for each selection have been added by us for differentiation. They are placed in parentheses.[3]

Selections from
"SAYINGS AND ADVICE"
(Maqūlāt-o Andarz-hā)

* * *

(Free from All...)

Know God according to His Value (qadr),
not according to the reasoning of people.
Know His Attributes according to His Worth,
not according to the conception of people.

Know His Power (tawān) according to His Value,
not according to the schemes of people.

He is existent as One,
distinct from what is imagined, (and)
free of all qualification.[4]

* * *

(Both Said the Truth)

Both said the truth.
The one who said. "One cannot know (Him)":
this is knowing the Reality (ḥaqīqat) of God.
And the one who said, "One can know (Him)":
this is common knowledge, that
there is no divinity but Him,
He has no partner,
He has none similar (to Him),
He has no need,
there is no comparison (ta<u>sh</u>bīh– with Him),
(and) there is no pause (ta'ṭīl – in His being present).[5]

* * *

(No One Can Precede God)

The knower ('ārif) has earned yearning through finding,
not finding through yearning.
The obedient (muṭī') has earned worship through dedication (i<u>kh</u>lāṣ),
not dedication through worship (tā'at).
The disobedient ('āṣī) has earned blame through punishment,
not punishment through blame.
Since the devotee is subject to a preceding (sābiqa – decree),
there is, in his capacity, neither being able nor being unable.

In no condition can one precede God;
the one who thinks he can precede God,
has no knowledge of God.
One looks from Him toward himself,
not from oneself toward Him;
because the eye belongs to the First Seer,
and the heart (belongs) to the First Friend.[6]

* * *

(Accept the Evident)

Our faith comes through hearing (sam'–of the teaching),
not through the schemes (ḥīlat) of the intellect ('aql).
Our faith is based on acceptance (qabūl) and submission (taslīm),
not on interpretation (ta'wīl) and aberrations (taṣarruf).

If the heart says, "Why?"
say: " I am inclining toward the (Divine) Command (amr)."
If the intellect says, "How?"
answer: "I am a servant (banda – of God)."

Accept the evident (ẓāhir);
commit (be-sopār) to the hidden (bāṭin);
leave any new (muḥdaṯh – interpretation);
do not abandon the preceding (salaf) way.[7]

* * *

(The Gracious Ones)

The struggling ones (and) the ascetic ones
eat simple food (and) wear coarse garments.
Those who have reached (the stage of) knowing (God)
do not go along but with gentle and amiable ones;
they do not become familiar but with gracious ones.[8]

* * *

(Bearing His Imprint)

All over the earth
there is no one more unworthy
than the one who feels secure in being worthy (bāyesta).
There is no one more unclean
than the one who thinks he is (perfectly) washed.

Two things are required:
neediness (neyāz) expressed by you (and)
help (yārī) from Him.

The needy one (coming to Him) is never dismissed;
there is no "but" (magar) beyond the wall of neediness (neyāz).

The favorite one ('azīz) bears His imprint (dāgh) upon him;
the one travelling toward Him takes His lamp (cherāgh).with him.[9]

* * *

(No Sleeping)

Sleeping is forbidden to the friends,
in this world and in the Hereafter:
in the Hereafter, because of the joy of union;
in this world, because of the grief of separation.
In Paradise there is no sleeping,
because of delight in seeing (Him).
In (this) world there is no sleeping (of the heart),
because of worries about remaining in the veil (ḥijab – of heedlessness).[10]

* * *

(Pursuit of the Friend)

The heart left,
and the Friend is (also) gone.
I don't know whether I should go after the Friend
or after the heart!
A voice spoke to me:
"Go in pursuit of the Friend,
because the lover needs a heart
in order to find union with the Friend.
If there was no Friend,
what would (the lover) do with (his) heart?"[11]

* * *

(The Beauty of Oneness)

Any eye filled with the vision of this world
cannot see the attributes of the Hereafter.
Any eye filled with the attributes of the Hereafter
would be deprived of the Beauty (Jamāl) of (Divine) Oneness.[12]

* * *

(In Each Breath)

O you who have departed from your own self,
and who have not yet reached the Friend:

do not be sad, (for)
He is accompanying you in each of (your) breaths.[13]

* * *

(The Divine Gaze)

There are two gazes: the human and the Divine;
the human gaze, when you see (only) yourself (and)
the Divine gaze, when God looks at you.
As long as the human gaze does not leave you,
the Divine gaze will not descend into your heart.

O miserable one (miskīn),
since your devotions are flawed,
why are you (proudly) looking at them (and)
what value can you give them
at the courtyard of the One who is Without Need (Ghanī)?

Don't you know that,
if you put the devotions of all the righteous ones on earth
next to the devotions of the angels in the heavens,
all this would not have the weight of a gnat
in the balance of the Most Glorious?[14]

* * *

(The Call of God)

The call of God is of three kinds:
He called some by the call of warning,
expressing His Magnitude;
the devotee fell in fear.
He called some by the call of glad tidings,
expressing the blessing of His Mercy;
the devotee fell in hope.
He called some by the call of kindness,
expressing His Felicity;
the devotee fell in longing.
The devotee must rotate between these three states:
fear, which prevents him from sin;
hope, which keeps him in (a state of) devotion; (and)
love, which saves him from his own self.

(Verse)

As long as you are (busy) with your own self,
You will not be admitted to (the way to) God.
Once you are free of your own self,
You will not be deprived of (His) regard (dīda).[15]

* * *

(To Offer the Soul)

To seek Paradise,
one has to try hard up to (the time of) death.
To escape Hell,
one has to practice austerity.
To seek the Friend,
one has to offer the soul (jān).

O my dear (novice):
Because of the Friend's severity (jafā),
escaping from the Friend would result in (a greater) severity.

According to the laws of friendship,
it would be wrong (for the lover)
to liberate (his) life and soul (jān) from the Friend.[16]

* * *

(Three Stages)

Here, there are three stages:
First, a flash of lightning from the heaven of (spiritual) poverty (faqr), in order to make you aware.
Second, a breeze from the air of humility (maskanat), in order to make you a confidant.
Third, a gate opened toward knowledge (ma'rifat – of God),
in order to make you a friend
and to clothe you with a robe of honor,
so that you may be a bold confidant![17]

* * *

(The Earner and the Knower)

The account (<u>sh</u>omār – of good and bad) in the Hereafter
concerns the earners (mozdūrān).
How does (this) account
concern the knower ('ārif — of God)?
The knower is a guest;

the earning of the earner and graciousness toward the knower
concern the Host (Mēzbān)!
The capital (māya) of the earner (mozdūr) is perplexity (ḥayrat)
and the capital of the knower is evident ('ayān).
The soul of the knower is compensation (tāwān) for His Love;
his soul is all eye,
his secret (sirr) is all tongue,
(and) both eye and tongue are helpless in the manifest Light.

The light of hope penetrates the heart of the earner, (and)
the manifest ('ayān) light penetrates the soul of the knower.
The earner will be moving among favors (ni'mat)
(and) the knower's state will be indescribable by means of words.

The value of the knower's breath (nafas) is inestimable,
a breath which is not distant from the (Divine) Presence (Ḥaḍrat).
(That) breath's origin is in the Presence and its destination is the Presence;
the knower's breath is a fire kindled by (God's) Friendship.[18]

* * *

(Remembrance)

The remembrance (dhikr – of God) is not only
what you bring forth on your tongue;
True remembrance is that
which you have deep in your soul.
The Unity (tāwḥīd – of God) is not only
what you know about His Oneness;
True Unity is to be one (yagāna) in regard to Him
and to be a stranger (bē-gāna) to what is not Him![19]

* * *

(The Three Beverages)

Anyone who enters through the door of agreement and submission
is given one of three beverages:
A beverage of knowledge (of God),
so that his heart may become alive with truth (ḥaqq).
A beverage of poison,
potent enough to wipe out the self (nafs)

which incites (to evil — Q. 12:53).

Or a beverage by means of which

the soul may become intoxicated and amazed:

thereby it may begin to discover

the truth,

the intimacy of (God's) company,

the savor of prayers, (and)

the sweetness of worship;

and (thereby) it may have the delight of knowledge (ma'rifat),

reach the spirit of intimate invocations (munājāt),

and become engaged in an occupation that is indescribable,

so that its whole life may be invaded by it.

(Verse)

You are not without me,
But I do not see Your Face.
You are the Soul,
With me, but Invisible![20]

* * *

(Friends and Friendships)

This life and the Hereafter

were both dedicated to friendship (dōstī).

And friendship

was dedicated to the Friend (Dōst).

Now, I wouldn't dare to say, "(Here) He is (Ō-st)!"

(Quatrain)

My eyes are filled with the picture (ṣūrat) of the Friend
(And) I am blessed by my eyes, since the Friend is there.
(But) to distinguish between the eyes and the Friend would not be correct,
Because either He is instead of the eyes, or He is the eyes![21]

* * *

(Beginning of Friendship)

The way to find friendship

is to toss this world and the Hereafter into the sea.

The sign of the realization of friendship

is to not take care of anything that is not God.

The beginning of friendship is having an imprint (dāgh);
the end is (having) a lamp (cherāgh).
The beginning of friendship is uneasiness (iḍtirār),
the middle of it is expecting (intiẓār)
(and) the end of it (is) seeing (dīdār).[22]

* * *

(Sign of Friendship)

The sign of acquiring the response of friendship
is contentment (riḍā).
That which increases the splendor of friendship
is devotion (wafā).
The principal fund of the treasure of friendship
is light (nūr).
The fruit of the tree of friendship
is delight (surūr).
The one who dissociates himself from this world and the Hereafter
is justified by friendship.
The one who solicits from the Friend any (gift) but the Friend
is ungrateful. (nā-sepās).
Friendship is friendship with (Divine) Truth (Ḥaqq–and)
all the rest is temptation (waswās).[23]

* * *

(Friendship is Eternal)

"He loves them and they love Him" (Q.5:54)
is a great matter (kār) and a magnificent bargain (bāzār) for the (man of) water and clay who became the pole of God's friendship;
the arrow of union is aimed at him, (and)
the devotee cannot be but delighted at this.
The state nearest to the Master is friendship;
the tree which brings forth the fruit of delight is friendship;
the beverage whose poison is all honey is friendship;
the path whose dust is all musc and ambergris is friendship;
the recording (raqam) of friendship is pre-eternal (azalī); (and)
the imprint (dāgh) of friendship is eternal. (abadī).[24]

* * *

(Nothing Can Be Said)

He, by Himself (<u>Dh</u>āt), is not (situated) in the heart:
in the heart is His remembrance (yād),
in the head is His love (mehr), (and)
in the soul is His overseeing (niẓẓāra).

The beginning of contemplation (mu<u>sh</u>āhda)
is vision (dīdār) by means of the heart:
then comes nearness (qurb) of the heart;
then comes finding (wujūd) by means of the heart
then comes (direct) observation (mu'āyana) by means of the heart;
then comes fading (istihlāk) of the heart in the Manifest ('ayān);
and beyond that, nothing can be said![25]

* * *

(His Early Grace)

Look for nearness,
so that intimacy emerges.
Look for magnificence,
so that reverence may increase.
Be waiting between this and that,
expecting whatever comes from (His) primordial (pre-eternal) Grace.[26]

* * *

(Contemplation of the Hidden)

Anyone who has done contemplation (mu<u>sh</u>āhada) of the hidden (bāṭin),
will not be ready for his tongue to express it,
or for his outward (ẓāhir – "being") to be aware of it.[27]

* * *

(Keep Silent)

A time will come when the tongue will join the heart,
the heart will join the soul (jān),
the soul will join the secret (sirr –consciousness),
and the secret will join the Truth (Ḥaqq).
The heart will say to the tongue, "Keep silent!"
The secret will say to the soul, "Keep silent!"
(And) the (inward) light (nūr) will say to the secret, "Keep silent!"[28]

* * *

(Morning Is Near)

O seekers:
Hurry up
O night travelers:
Don't go to sleep, (for) the morning is near.
O hurring ones:
Be steadfast, (for) the station is near.
O thirsty ones:
Be patient, (for) the spring is near.
O strangers:
Be gratified, (for) the Host is near.
O (you who are) looking for the friends (of God):
Be delighted, (for) the welcome is near.[29]

* * *

(Beatitude)

To reject everything
is the sign of the nearness (qurb) of the Friend.
Your "being" (būd) is a costly expense (tāwān) for you;
if you forsake your "being,"
that will be your eternal delight and blessing.[30]

* * *

(Unification)

Unification (tawhīd) is not only
to know Him as One:
real unification is to be (dedicated) to only Him,
and to sever (ties) with all except Him.
The beginning of (God's) favour to them (the lovers)
is to give them a resolve (qaṣd) from the unseen (g̲h̲aybī),
so that they may be severed from the world;
once isolated (fard),
they will deserve union (wiṣāl) with the Singular One (Fard).
O God,
Your seeker must be like You, a singular one (fard),
free from all flaws and failures.[31]

NOTES

1. In the Murād Mollā Library of Istanbūl, dated: 852/1448 C.E.
2. See the Preliminary Notes for the "Intimate Invocations."
3. We have done the same for the "Intimate Invociation" (Munājāt) in the next section. These titles, in spite of being drawn from the words and themes of the texts, do not exist in the original Darī-Persian texts.
4. Kashf al-Asrār, Vol. 2, p.507.
5. Kashf al-Asrār, Vol.5, p. 584.
6. Kashf al-Asrār, Vol. 10, p. 35.
7. K.A., Vol. 6, p. 310.
8. K.A., Vol. 3, p. 484 (text is in Arabic).
9. K.A.., Vol. 7. p. 92.
10. K.A.., Vol. 7, p. 540.
11. K.A.., Vol. 1, p. 628.
12. K.A.., Vol. 7, p. 511.
13. K.A.., Vol. 7, p. 268.
14. K.A.., Vol. 8, p. 57.
15. K.A.., Vol. 4, p. 131.
16. K.A.., Vol. 6, p. 424.
17. K.A.., Vol. 4, p. 168.
18. K.A.., Vol. 7, p. 152.
19. K.A.., Vol. 2, p. 396.
20. K.A.., Vol. 3, p. 543.
21. K.A.., Vol. 1, p. 31. The word for "eyes" is singular (dīda) in theoriginal Persian.
22. K.A.., Vol. 7, p. 513.
23. K.A.., Vol. 3, p. 155.
24. K.A.., Vol. 3, p. 155.
25. K.A.., Vol. 7, p. 91.
26. K.A.., Vol. 7, p. 437.
27. K.A.., Vol. 6, p. 478.
28. K.A.., Vol. 6, p. 389.
29. K.A.., Vol. 3, p. 610.
30. K.A.., Vol. 6, p. 389.
31. K.A.., Vol. 4, p. 267.

THE INTIMATE INVOCATIONS

(MUNĀJĀT)

BY 'ABDULLĀH ANṢĀRĪ OF HERĀT

(1006-1089 C.E.)

Selected texts translated from the original Darī-Persian

PRELIMINARY NOTES

The "Inimate Invocations" are the most well-known sayings of 'Abdullāh Anṣārī in Darī-Persian.

The Arabic word "munājāt" (radicals, NJY, NJW) means "intimate and confidential conversion."[1] The common meaning of "Munājāt" in Persian is "intimate invocations to God," "inward converse with God." "fervent prayer (sometimes silent, sometimes chanted)," "sincere and open-hearted prayer."

The "Invocations" of Abdullāh Anṣārī have a few characteristic of Quranic style and are in rhymed prose (saj'), without being poetry. The aesthetic and psychological effects of such assonance are, unfortunately, lost in the translation (a well-known outcome of rhymed texts that are translated from one language to another). These "Invocations" in rhymed prose are the main reason for the great popularity of Anṣārī among Persian-speaking peoples. Numerous editions entitled "Book of (Invocations to) God" ("Elāhī Nāma")[2] are continually being written by the best calligraphers and printed commercially in Iran, Afghānistān, and Pākistān.

As we explained in the beginning of Part Two, the texts of this group of printed booklets are not completely authenticated by the earliest available manuscripts. It would, however, be imprudent to reject these popular and commercial pamphlets in their entirety, insofar as their style and, in some cases, their contents, are not far from the genuine invocations incorporated in the "Commentary on the Qur'an" (Kashf al-Asrār) and the "Generations of the Sūfīs" (Ṭabaqāt al-Ṣūfiyya). In some cases, the phrases in the popular editions are simplified versions of early manuscripts. However, in spite of these stylistic and substantial similarities between the early compilations and the later manuscripts, some scholars[3] do not accept the authenticity of the later invocations attributed to Anṣārī, which according to them, cannot be genuine. On the other hand, the frequent linguistic "archaisms" of the early compilations make some of the passages difficult for the readers of today to understand in regard to phonetics, morphology, and semantics. Even if the late manuscripts were based on earlier sources, unknown to us today, they must have been "modernized" for the sake of the 15th century (C.E.) readers, (See page 19 to 23).

Table F

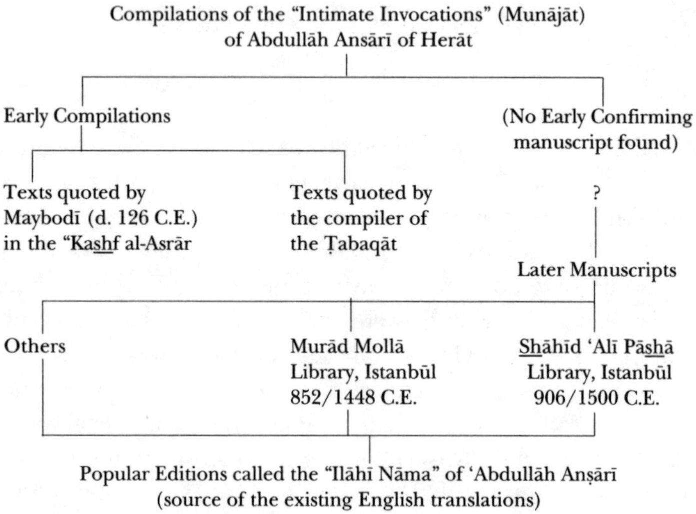

The fact remains that these popular editions of the "Invocations" have exerted, for several centuries, a great impact upon the devotees of Sufism, many of whom are unconnected to any particular Ṣūfī order (ṭarīqat). This is a major socio-cultural observation when we study the image of Anṣārī among Persian-speaking peoples from Shīrāz to Bokhāra, or non-Persian-speaking admirers from Delhi to Istanbūl. All the available English translations are based on these commercial popular editions.[4]

Translations from the earlier manuscripts are only available in French.[5]

Variants of many of the texts of the invocations incorporated in the "Commentary on the Qur'an" are also found in the "Generations." Some of the invocations in the "Generations" have been recorded in Darī-Persian texts which are full of archaisms and based on unclearly written manuscripts.

In this section we have translated some of the invocations found in the volumes of "Commentary on the Qur'an" together with some from the "Generations." We have not translated the invocations found in later manuscripts or in popular editions.

A translation into English of all the genuine invocations available in these two works remains to be done.

Selections from "THE INTIMATE INVOCATIONS" (Munājāt)

* * *

(Where Are You?)

O God,
You are the aim of the call of the sincere,
You enlighten the souls of the friends, (and)
You are the comfort of the hearts of the travellers—
because You are present in the very soul.

I call out, from emotion:
"Where are You?"

You are the life of the soul,
You are the rule (āyīn) of speech, (and)
You are Your own interpreter (tarjamān).

For the sake of Your obligation to Yourself,
do not enter us into the shade of deception, (but)
make us reach union (wiṣāl) with You.[6]

* * *

(Beyond Imagination)

O God,
You are beyond imagination,
above the perceptions of intellects,
beyond assumptions, and
not found by the eyes.
You provide liberation
to those who meet hardships.

You provide joy
to those who are grieved.
There is no "why" about Your command,
there is no "how" about Your person (Dhāt),
(and) there is no "similar to" about Your attributes.[7]

* * *

(I Seek Refuge In You)

O God,
I seek refuge (in You) from two claims
and I ask Your help and kindness in complaining about both claims:
first, if I believe I have achieved something by myself;
second, if I believe I have any rights in regard to You.[8]

* * *

(Only You)

O God,
Look to three things about me:
first, prostrations directed by the heart for You only;
second, affirmations, (when) I said "That is right!"
to anything You said;
third, when the breeze of (Your) generosity blew,
(my) heart and soul did not cherish (anyone) but You.[9]

* * *

(Who Can Know You?)

O God,
Who can know You?
Since (only) You know Yourself,
no one knows You.
O You, who worthy of Your own praise!
O You, who are thankful for Your own gifts!

The devotee, by himself, is unable to serve and worship You;
by his own intellect, he is unable to appreciate Your Graciousness;
by his entirety, he is unable to be delight in Your company;
(and)

by his power, he is unable to perform what is proper to You.

O Generous One,
I am suffering from an illness the remedy of which is You, (and)
I am dedicated to a praise worthy of You!
You know what I know about You:
You are the One (about whom) You said, " I am That,"
and You are That![10]

* * *

(You Are All)

O God,
You know everything,
You achieve every task, (and)
You sustain everyone.

No one can compete with You (and)
No one is free from needing you.
With Wisdom, You conduct affairs (and)
with Gracefulness (Luṭf), You conclude them.
There is no injustice, no amusement, and no games (bāzī).

O God,
The (human) servant has no knowledge of the nature of Your affairs;
no one has authority (ḥukm) over You.
You established everything suitable to everyone;
You decide on (Your) favors.
No one is connected to You (and)
You are not connected to any one.
Everything is from You to You;
You are All, and that is all (bas.)[11]

* * *

(The Life of the Universe)

O God,
You are found (mawjūd) by knowers ('ārifān),
You are the objective of the hearts of longing ones, (and)
You are recalled by the tongues of praising ones.

How could I not call to you,
when You are the One Who listens to those praying?

How could I not praise You,
when You are the One who bestows delight
to the hearts of devotees?

How could I not recognize You,
when You are the (Creator) of this world?

How could I not love You,
when You are the Life of the Universe?[12]

* * *

(To Praise You)

O You,
Worthy of Your own praise.
O You,
Thanking Yourself for Your own favors.
O You,
Representing your trials as being agreeable.
The devotee, by himself, is unable to praise You;
with his intellect, he is unable to suitably appreciate You; (and)
With his means, he is unable to properly serve You.
O Generous One,
I am the captive of the pain for which You are the remedy.
I humbly admire the praise that You deserve;
You know what I know about You.
You are the One that You described;[13]
You are as You said.
This is how Muḥammad spoke his invocation;
"I cannot enumerate the praises You deserve;
You are as You praise Yourself."[14]

* * *

(As You Have Said)

O God,
People indicate how near You are,
but You are more lofty than that.
People think how far You are,
but You are much closer than the soul.

You are found (mawjūd) in the spirits of Your champions, (for)
You are present (ḥāḍir) in the hearts of those
who mention Your Name.

O King,
You are the one (about) whom You have spoken;
and as You have said,
You are that (very) one![15]

* * *

(Your Radiance)

O God,
Your Radiance
has enlightened the lamp of knowledge (ma'rifat);
my heart is nothing.
Your Witnessing
is my interpreter;
my speech is nothing.
Your Nearness (qurb)
has enlightened the lamp of finding (wajd);
my resolution (himmat) is nothing.
Your Will (irādat)
has settled my affairs;
my effort (jahd) is nothing.
Your Being (būd)
has satisfied my need;
my being is nothing
O God,
What did I gain from my being,
except ordeals (balā') and distress ('anā);
while Your Being
is all Gift ('aṭā') and Fulfillment (wafā').
O You,
Who are manifest through Kindness (and)
evident through Generosity:
view the actions of (this) devotee as not done,
and do what suits You![16]

* * *

(The Guide Toward You)

O God,
You inspire speech in those devotees who make intimate invocations,
You bring intimacy (uns) to those who recall You in solitude (khalwat,)
(and) You dwell in the breaths (nafas) of those who keep Your secrets.
We have no company but the recollection of You,
we have no provision (while travelling) but remembrance of You, (and)
we have no guide toward You but You.
O God,
Look at the need of the one
who has no need but from the One.[17]

* * *

(The Seeds of Guidance)

O God,
By Your primordial (pre-eternal) Compassion,
You sowed the seeds of guidance;
by sending prophets as messengers,
You irrigated those seeds;
by Your assistance and bounty, You grew them (and)
by Your regard, You enabled them to bear fruit.

O God,
It is suitable that You protect them from the hot sandstorm
of (Your) coercion (qahr),
and that You nurture the seeds sown by Your pre-eternal bounty
with Your eternal care.[18]

* * *

(Except You)

O You,
You sow (the seeds) of repentance in the hearts
of those who are acquainted (āshnā), (and)

You send a burning fervor (sōz) into the hearts
of those who are repentant.
O You,
You give admission to the sinners and those who confess.
No one returned to You
unless You rescued him.
No one found the way (to You)
unless You took his hand.

Take (our) hands,
because there is no one else to take hands.
Help (us) (dar-yāb),
because there is no refuge except You.
There is no answer to our request except You
there is no remedy to our pains except You, (and)
there is no relief for our sorrow except You.[19]

* * *

(Drown in the Fire)

I know the pitcher,
but I won't attempt to drink (from it).
(My) heart is thirsty (and)
I am longing for a drop.
The (caravan's) water jug is not enough for me, (since)
I'm seeking the ocean.

How many fountains and streams have I passed,
So that (one day) I might discover the Ocean.

Have you ever seen someone drowning in a fire?
That is what I am (doing).
Have you ever seen someone dying of thirst in a lake?
That is what I am (doing).

Certainly I am like someone bewildered in a desert
and I keep calling out, "Help!"
I cry out because my heart has been carried off.[20]

* * *

(The Ocean of Bewilderment)

O God,
You kindly became manifest (paydā)
to Your friends,
You exhilarated them
with the wine of intimacy (uns),
and You drowned some of the others
in the ocean of bewilderment (dah<u>sh</u>at).
You raised Your call from very near,
and You dispatched the signal from far away.
You summoned the devotee,
and You hid Yourself.
You exposed Yourself from behind the veil,
and You menifested Yourself with the signs of Magnificence,
until You caused those knights (jawān-mardān)
to be lost in the valley of bewilderment
and to be wandering and exhausted.
Why have You done all this to those unlucky ones?
You will be the Judge for those plaintiffs!
You will award justice to those imploring ones!
You will be the blood atonement for those slain ones!
You will be the Savior of those drowned ones!
(And) You will be the Guide of those lost ones:
until the lost ones can find the way,
the drowned ones can reach the shore,
and those exhausted souls can rest!
When will the answer to their mysterious story come?
(And) when will the night of their waiting reach the morning
(light)?[21]

* * *

(Blessed Be This Pain)

O God,
In all this affair,
the lot of this destitute one
is only pain (dard).
May this pain be blessed, (for)
it is very suitable to me!

Anyone deprived of this pain
 is unfortunate (bē-chāra).
Anyone is unmanly (nā-jawān-mard)
 who is not proud of having this pain![22]

* * *

(The Victory)

How could I have known
 that the mother of joy is sorrow,
 and that under every misfortune
 a thousand treasures are hiding?

How could I have known
 that desire is the bringer of Union,
 and that beneath the cloud of Munificence
 despair is impossible?

How could I have know
 that the Possessor of Majesty
 is so comforting toward (His) devotees,
 and that the friends (of God)
 are so much favored by Him?

How could I have known
 that what I am searching for
 is in the midst of the soul,
 and that the honor of Your Union
 is for me an opening and victory?

(Quatrain)

Once in my life, when the night became morning,
The image (khayāl) of the soul of Peace came to me
 And asked me, "What happened to you, O wounded one?"
I said, "From love for You, this victory (futūḥ) was given to me."[23]

* * *

(The Day You Were Mine)

O God,
If some found You by seeking,
 I found (You) by escaping (from myself).

If some found You by remembering,
    I found You by forgetting (myself).
If some found You by desiring,
    I found desiring (for You) from You!

O God,
You are the means of access to Yourself:
    You were the First One (and)
    You will be the Last One.
All is You, and that is all (bas),
    (and) the rest is (only) fancy (hawas).

O God,
How will I find again the Day (when)
        You were mine,
        and I was not.
    Until I find that Day again,
        I will be in fire and smoke.

If I find that Day,
    (even) at the cost of this world and the Hereafter,
    I will be in the (greatest) gain.
And if I find myself in Your Being;
    I will be content in my non-being.[24]

* * *

(Will I Live That Day?)

O God,
You made (me) pass over a thousand steep paths ('aqaba),
    (and now) One is left..
My heart is ashamed
    of having called so much for Your (help).

O God,
You washed (me) with a thousand waters,
    in order to acquaint (me) with (Your) Friendship (dōstī).
One washing is left:
    so that You may wash me
        from me;
    so that I may rise from my "self",
        and only You may stay!

O God,
Will I live that Day when,
without my own efforts,
I may open my eyes
and not see my "self" in front of me?[25]

* * *

(The Grace of God)

Lord,
The one whom You do not desire, how can he come?
The one whom You do not call will never come.
What response is there for the one whom You have not called?
What (purpose) is water to a field left fallow?
What benefit is sweet water if the plant is bitter?
What profit does the thorn get from perfume of the rose?

Yes, lineage is the lineage of piety,
and the family tie is the tie of the Faith.
Muḥammad made a family tie for Salmān (because of his) piety and connected him to himself.
He said:
"Salmān is ours, a member of (our) family (ahlu 'l-bayt)."
Yet Abū Lahab (the enemy of Faith) was the uncle of the Messenger!
See, than, what benefit was Quraysh ancestry for him,
and to be of the clan of the Messenger?
All this is so that you may know
that the affair depends upon His favor
and not lineage or ties of blood.[26]

* * *

(Your Bounties)

O God,
If You bestow on me Your bounties,
I do not mind the unjust "justice" of others.
For when You administer justice,
the bounties of others are (as cheap as) wind.

O God,
What I was given by You

can adorn this world and the Hereafter.
Strangely, my soul is scared
by the fear of Your justice![27]

* * *

(The Gratified Ones)

O God,
How cherished is the one whom You want,
(for) if he escapes, You come on his way!
How pleased is the one for whom You are his;
I wonder whose You are from among us![28]

* * *

(Free Us From Ourselves)

Everything I considered as a sign
was finally revealed to be only a veil.
Everything I recognized as a resource
was finally revealed to the useless.

O God,
Remove at once this veil,
and make me free of the flaws of my "being",
and do not leave me as the hostage of my own efforts.

O God,
Do not let us be surrounded by our own acts,
and free us from our self-inflicted damages.
O Almighty, the Merciful,
Maintain what You have made without us,
without our interventions, (and)
do not leave us to handle what You Yourself have woven.[29]

* * *

(Recall Us)

O God,
How can I recall (yād)
(when) I am myself entirely recall (yād).
I have scattered in the wind the harvest of my own signs,
(so) how can I recall the One I did not forget?

O Memorial (yādgār) of souls,
Remembered of hearts,
and Recalled by tongues:
through Your mercy, recall us, (and)
make us delighted with the kindness of Your recalling.[30]

* * *

(I Came to Your Court)

O God,
Sometimes You say, "Come in!"
And at times You say, "Be careful!"

O God,
Is all this a sign of nearness (qurbat),
or (is it) only furor and upheaval?
Because I have never seen glad tidings
accompanied so much by threats and warnings!

O Merciful and Forbearing,
O Kind and Beneficent,
I came to Your Court:
it is up to You to treat me with Your bounty,
or to handle me with sternness.[31]

* * *

(To Observe You)

O God,
You blended the fire of finding (yāft),
with the Light of knowing (<u>sh</u>enā<u>kh</u>t).
You showered the rain of singularity (fardāniyyat),
on the dust of humanity (ba<u>sh</u>ariyyat).
With the fire of friendship,
You burned up (human) water-and-clay,
to enable the (devotee's) eye of knowing
to observe (dīdār — You).[32]

* * *

(To Reach You)

O God,
Those whom You have chosen searched for You by You;
they are reunited (with You).

Those whom you have not chosen, searched for You by themselves;
they are severed from You.
He who is reunited will not know how to express gratitude,
(and) he who is severed will not know how to express regrets.

O You who causes one to reach You,
and who are reached by You (alone):
cause me to reach (You),
since no one can reach (you) by himself.[33]

* * *

(The Discovered)

O God,
By what means shall I seek You?
Because (only) You exist, and that is all.
Nothing (else is) in front of me and
nothing (else) beyond You!

Whatever I may seek
is more worthless than myself.
Finding You is greater
than (any) sign (nishān) and time (hangām).

In Your kingdom, the world is less than a hair;
while You are Manifest,
what would it mean to seek you?

The one seeking You (jōyenda-é tū) is (only) the companion of himself;
to seek Being (hast) by means of non-being (nēst)
is the fancy of "drunkards!"

To find You involves neither time (hangām) nor means (sabab);
the one who is dependent on seeking (ṭalab) is veiled (maḥjūb).
To seek You is a remnant of separation and dispersion:
You are before everything,
(so) what (would it mean) to seek you?

To seek Unity through duality is being lost;
to be bound to the path of seeking (ṭalab) is misfortune.

All things except One are the same;
being (hast) is One (yakī),
and other things are less than nothing.

The one who keeps seeking the Discovered (mawjūd) is lost,
(for) the Truth (Ḥaqq) is more evident (ma'lūm) than the seeker;
therefore, there is no seeking and no seeker.

Tear (away) the veil,
for God is manifest (paydā)!
The Discovered (yāfta) is a sufficient sign (nishān)
for what is to be found (yāft).
In the eye of Unification,
there is no one except the Single (fard)![34]

* * *

(What Shall I Discover?)

Any one who said "I found You!"
has to be delivered from himself.
The Present cannot be sought by the absent,
nor the Existent (hast) by the non-existent.
Anyone who found You has seen You (torā dīd),
and anyone who has seen You
has ceased to see himself.

I am a veil to myself,
I am in torment from myself, (and)
I am hurrying uselessly.

What shall I discover (then),
once I cease to be![35]

* * *

(A Way to Explain)

O God,
What I have discovered (mawjūd-é man)
couldn't be borne by my heart
or (said) by my speech.
Have you heard about a borrowed ('āriyyat) discovery?
That is my case!

This (saying) "I" and "me" is defective,
but in expressing these words, I am a translator (tarjamān).
Every "I" that I pronounce is false (zūr),
but I lack the means (ḥīlat)
to give (any other) indication to the listener.[36]

* * *

(Toward Union)

O God,
Since I learned (āmōkhtam) what must be learned,
I have burned all that I learned.
I have thrown away what I treasured (andōkhta),
and what I threw away, I have (now) treasured (back) again.
I have sold everything void of being (nēst)
in order to enlighten (afrōkhtan) everything that has real being (hast).

O God,
Since I have learned about Union (yagānagī),
I am longing, in my fondness, for (that) delight (shādī).
The time will come when I will say:
I have thrown away the measure (paymāna — for doing business),
I have severed all (worldly) links, (and)
I have lost and undone my being (būd)!

(Verse)
When will it be
That I may open this cage,
So that I may make my nest
In the Garden of God (bāgh-é Elāhī)?[37]

* * *

(The Speaker Speaks)

If I am the one who speaks,
may my tongue be dried up
so it can become silent!
If I am the one who hears,
may my ears be deaf
So they cannot be blamed.

Therefore, it is not me:
the Speaker Himself speaks;
The Hearer Himself hears![38]

* * *

(The Friend Beside Me)

O God
You know why I am happy:
It is because I seek Your company,
not through my own (efforts).

O God,
You decided and I did not.
I found the Friend beside me
when I woke up![39]

* * *

(This Festival)

There was a time I was looking for Him
and I was finding my "self".
Now I look for myself
and I find Him!

O You (who are) reminder (yād) of evidence (ḥujjat),
(and) O You (who are) the memorial (yādgār) of intimacy (uns):
While You are Present,
what is the use of searching?
While I have,
why should I look?
While I see,
what should I say?

I am in love with this (kind of) seeking (and)
I am captivated by this whole story.

O You who precede any day and
Who are distinct from anyone:
For this festival (sūr),
a thousand musicians would not suffice me![40]

NOTES

1. The word "munājāt" has the same root as "najwā", "private discourse" or "secret talk" (Q.17:47: 20:62; 21:3; 58:7-10). It is also closely related to the word "najīy" in the verse, "And We called him (Moses) from the right side of Mount (Sinai) and made him draw near to Us for mystic converse" (Q.19:52, Yūsuf 'Alī's translation). It has also been translated as "communion" (Muḥammad 'Alī, Pickthall, Arberry, Shākir), and "mystic communion" (Asad).
2. They have the word "Elāhī" because the invocations (munājāt) begin with this word, which means "O God!" The editions themselves begin with the words, which means "O Generous One, the Bestower of Gifts" (Ay Karīm-ē ke Bakhshenda-yé 'Atā'ī).
3. Including the late Ṣalāḥu-d-dīn Saljūqī, who spoke to the author in 1955 in Cairo, and S. de Laugier de Beaurecueil.
4. See Bibliography.
5. See Beaurecueil's "Cris du Coeur."
6. Kashf al-Asrār, Vol., 5, p. 598.
7. Kashf al-Asrār, Vol., 7, p. 436.
8. Kashf al-Asrār, Vol., 4, p. 122.
9. K.A., Vol., 4, p. 107.
10. K.A., Vol., 1, p. 30.
11. K.A., Vol., 7, p. 337.
12. K.A., Vol., 3. p. 470.
13. Means: You are the One that You described in the Qur'an.
14. K.A., Vol., 3, p. 808. This Tradition (ḥadīth) in Arabic is: "lā aḥṣā thanā'a 'alayka; anta kamā athnayta 'alā nafsik."
15. K.A., Vol., 1, p. 498.
16. K.A., Vol., 1, p. 28.
17. K.A., Vol., 7, p. 583.
18. K.A., Vol., 6, p. 19.
19. K.A., Vol., 6, p. 494.
20. K.A., Vol., 1, p. 413. The word translated as "lake" (daryā), literally means "sea", and here refers to an inland sea of freshwater.
21. K.A., Vol., 6, p. 528.
22. K.A., Vol., 7, p. 439.
23. K.A., Vol., 2, p. 445.
24. K.A., Vol., 3, p. 122.
25. K.A., Vol., 7, p. 398.
26. K.A., Vol., 3, p. 106.
27. K.A., Vol., 5, p. 623.
28. K.A., Vol., 1, p. 29.
29. K.A., Vol., 7, p. 41.
30. K.A., Vol., 9, p. 833.
31. K.A., Vol., 4, p. 358.

32. K.A., Vol., 4, p. 168.
33. K.A., Vol., 1, p. 699.
34. Ṭabaqāt al-Ṣūfīyya, p. 178.
35. Ṭabaqāt al-Ṣūfīyya, p. 178.
36. Ṭabaqāt al-Ṣūfīyya, p. 333.
37. K.A., Vol., 4, p. 347.
38. Ṭabaqāt al-Ṣūfīyya, p. 333.
39. K.A., Vol., 5, p. 407.
40. K.A., Vol., 6, p. 17.

Appendix A

CHRONOLOGY

'Abdullāh Anṣārī's Life in Historical Perspective

A. Ages 1 to 10: Early Childhood (1006-1016 C.E.)

C.E. YEARS	AGE		HIJRA YEARS
		Sulṭān Maḥmūd of Ghazna was Emperor.	
1006	0		396
		Born, on the evening of May 4, 1006 C.E., Sha'bān 2, 396 H.	
1008	2		398
		His father, Abū-Manṣūr, a shop keeper in the Kohan-dezh ("old citadel") of Heart was a Ṣūfī who had spent long years of his youth in Balkh.	
1011	5		402
		'Abdullāh was put in a school run by a woman. Then sent to the Mālīnī school.	
		402/1011: military campaigns of Sulṭān Maḥmūd of Ghazna in India.	
1012	6		403
		Learned the reading of Qur'an taught to him by the muqri' (readers).	
1013	7		404
		403/1012: the death of Bahā al-Dawla and the decline of the Shī'a Būyīd Dynasty in Western Irān.	
		1013: the death of Bāqillānī, the systematizer of Ash'arī Kalām.	
1015	9		406
		His father, Abū-Manṣūr, and Jārūdī dictated ḥadīth tradition to him, at the age of nine.	

His father acted strangely by suddenly abandoning Herāt, his family and shop, and went to look for his Ṣūfī companions in Balkh.

B. Ages 11 to 19: A Precocious Teenager (1017-1025 C.E.)

1017 11 408

'Abdullāh also studied poetry under an "adīb" (well-read scholar). His daily practices: studying and memorizing Qur'an and ḥadīth; writing letters and poetry; studying at home; had little time to eat.

409/1018: Caliph al-Qādir prohibited the Kalām.

1019 13 (approximateive date) 410

Abandoned by the father, the family became destitute. It seems that some friends began to help the family. The education of 'Abdullāh was taken care of by:

1. A Ṣūfī: Shaykh 'Amū, who built a khānaqāh in the suburb of Herāt. 'Abdullāh was only 14 when the Shaykh designated him as his successor.
2. A commentator of Qur'an, Yaḥyā Ibn 'Ammār Shaybānī, an opponent of the Ash'arī "innovators". Ibn 'Ammār taught Quranic exegesis.
3. 'Abd-al-Jabbār Jarrāḥī, who taught him to read ḥadīth on the basis of the Jāmi' ("Collection") of Tirmidhī.
4. (later) Ṭāqī of Sejestān, a sensitive and pnetrating Ṣūfī master who was a Ḥanbali.

ca. 411/1020: the death of Ferdawsī of Ṭūs.

412/1021: the death of Abū-'Abd-al-Raḥmān al-Sulamī, the author of "Ṭabaqāt al-Ṣūfiyya" in Arabic.

1023 17 414

Continued his studies of Qur'an and ḥadīth and continued to be initiated to Sufism.

416/1025: the Seljuq Turks crossed the Oxus.

C. Ages 20 to 27: Toward Maturity (1026-1033 C.E.)

1026 20 417

Death of his spiritual mentor, Ṭāqī. 'Abdullāh went

to Nishāpūr to further study ḥadīth and to meet spiritual masters like Abū-Naṣr Manṣūr Aḥmad al-Mufassir, Abū-Sa'īd Sayrafī, Abū-l-Ḥasan Salīṭī. 'Abdullāh returned to Herāt after a few months.

1027 21 418

Active in the meetings of scholars of the ḥadīth.

1028 22 419

421/April 30, 1030: Sulṭān Maḥmūd died.

1030: death of Ibn-Miskawayh, philosopher and moralist.

421/1031: Sulṭān Mas'ūd I, Emperor in Ghazna.

Shaykh 'Amū made him director of the Khānaqāh.

1031 25 422

'Abdullāh's teacher of Quranic commentary, Yaḥyā b. 'Ammār Shaybānī, died.

1032 26 423

'Abdullāh offered to accompany the old Imām Abū'l-Faḍl b. Sa'd to Mecca for Ḥajj. The Khorāsānī caravan had to return from Baghdād because of the news of unsafe roads between Irāq and the Ḥijāz. In the spring of 1032, 'Abdullāh was back in Herāt.

1033 27 424

He tried again. He stayed in Nishāpūr in the Khānaqāh of Ibn Bākū and met the Ṣūfī Abū-Sa'īd b. Abū'l-Khayr who spoke to him about Kharaqānī. The caravan reached Rayy. Lack of security forced the caravan to return to Khorāsān. At Dāmghān, 'Abdullāh met the Ṣūfī Muḥammad Qaṣṣāb of Āmol.

His meeting with Kharaqānī, an encounter which changed his life.

By Nov. 1033, he was back in Herāt in the Khānaqāh of Shaykh 'Amū.

D. Ages 28 to 35: Beginnings of Teaching (1034-1041 C.E.)

425/1034: Seljuqs attained northern Khorāsān.

Sulṭān Mas'ūd came to Herāt.

1034 28 425

425/Winter 1034: ecstatic days of the meeting of Sufis in Nobādhān, south of Herāt. As a result of the Nobādhān meeting, Anṣārī decided to

cease participating in spiritual concerts (samā‘).
He opted for a Sufism of lucidity (ṣaḥw) instead of delirious and frenzied mysticism.

1036 30 427

He made a visit to Ṣūfī Shaykhs in Cheshth, at the upper Harī-rōd basin.

427/1036: death of Abū-Isḥāq al-Tha‘labī, commentator of Qur’an.

429/1037: death of Ibn-Sinā, philosopher.

1038: death of Abū-Ya‘qūb Qarrāb of Sarakhs, his master of ḥadīth. Anṣārī took charge of the teaching.

1038: the Seljuq army defeated the Ghaznavid army at Dandānaqān. Toghril proclaimed himself Sulṭān at Nishāpūr.

1038 32 429

Anṣārī summoned to Sulṭān Mas‘ūd’s court in Herāt.

1039 33 430

430/1039: Abū-Manṣūr, Anṣārī’s father, died in Balkh.
Anṣārī was accused by the Ash‘arites of anthropomorphism (tashbīh) and was summoned to the Court of Mas‘ūd in Herāt. His words assured the Sulṭān, who honored him.
Around this time, Anṣārī wrote “Al-Arba‘īn fī Dalā’il al-Tawḥīd” (Forty Traditions on the Divine Unity).

432/Jan.1, 1041: Sulṭān Mas‘ūd killed by his nephews in India. His son Mawdūd never succeeded in reconquering Khorāsān.

E. Ages 36 to 46: A Decade of Hardships (1042 - 1052 C.E.)

1041 35 433

433/1041 An assembly of theologians prohibited him to teach. He exiled himself to Shakīwān near Pōshanj (1041 to 1043).

1044 38 436

436/1044, Back in Herāt, he re-started the teaching of Quranic commentary.

1046 40 438

438/1046: Another assembly of theologians presented

a petition against Anṣārī. He was banished from Herāt and imprisoned in irons during five months in Pōshanj.

1047 41 439

Back in Herāt, he took up his Quranic commentary again the spent long periods of time in teaching the interpretation of Sūrah 2, verses 160-65, about those who are "the most ardent in their love of God."

440/1049: the death of Abū-Sa'īd b. Abi'l-Khayr, Ṣūfī poet.

1049 43 441

Nov. 30, 1049: Shaykh 'Amū, his generous and discreet caretaker died. For many years, Anṣārī, although well-dressed when teaching, used to live at home, in extreme poverty. His friends were unaware of his indigence.

F. Ages 47 to 57: A Decade of Achievements (1053 - 1063 C.E.)

445/1053: the Seljūk Sultan, Togrel Beg, agreeing with his secretary Kondorī, started to persecute Ash'arites, Anṣārī's major opponents.

1053 47 445

Anṣārī's reputation spread all over the Seljūkid and 'Abbasid Empires. Abū-l-Ḥasan of Bākharz and Abū'l-Qāsim al-Bāri' of Zōzan visited him.

1054 48 446

Friends became aware of his poverty at home and gifts were made to him.

1055 49 447

The judge, Abū'l-'Alā Saīd b. Sayyār, a Hanafite offered a place to him in the major mosque of Herāt to teach the Quranic commentary and to preach.

447/1055: Toghril entered Baghdād and the Caliph recognized his title of Sulṭān.

1056 50 448

448/1056-57: A student noted his dictation as "Sad Maydān" (The Hundred Grounds) in Darī-Persian, a mnemonic Ṣūfī manual.

450/1058: death of al-Māwardī, a jurist and pro-Caliph theoretician..

			("Al-Aḥkām al-Sulṭāniyya "— "The Principles of Government").	
1059	53			451
		450/1059: unsuccessful petitions by opponents to Alp Arslān for prohibiting Anṣārī's lectures.		
1060	54			452
		During these years, friends and devotees were supporting him. His material situation improved.		
1063	57			455
			455/1063: Alp Arslān, became the Seljūq Sulṭān. Niẓām-al-Mulk was appointed Vizier.	

G. Ages 58 to 64: Combating the Innovators (1064 - 1070 C.E.)

1064	58			456
		456/1064: Anṣārī's opponents tried to provoke a polemic with him in the presence of the Sulṭān and the Vizier. Anṣārī refused to discuss anything not based on the Qur'an and Sunnah.		
			456/1064: measures against the Ash'arites were abolished because of Niẓām-al-Mulk's policies.	
1066	60			458
		458/1066: Anṣārī's opponents obtained an expulsion order against him from the Vizier. Anṣārī was exiled to Balkh for a short time and was given permission to return to Herāt. The Vizier amended his policy and adopted a line in favor of the traditionalists.		
1068	62			460
		Anṣārī continued preaching in the Grand Mosque of Herāt, teaching Quranic commentary in his lectures, and guiding the Ṣūfī novices in the Khānaqāh.		
			460/1068: the death of Abū Ja'far of Tūs, the Shī'a commentator on the Qur'an	
1070	64			462
		462: A stratagem by the opponents (accusing Anṣārī to be an anthropomorphist) failed in the presence of Alp Arslān. 462/1069: The Caliph, al-Qā'im, upon the suggestion of Niẓām al-Mulk, sent him a robe of honor from Baghdād.		

H. Ages 65 to 78: Celebrity and Grandeur (1071 -1084 C.E.)

1071 65 463

Marzūq, Mu'tamin Sāji, and Muḥammad b. Ṭāhir Maqdisī were his intimates in the Khānaqāh.

ca. 1071: death of Hujwīrī, the author of "Kashf al-Maḥjūb," in Lahore.

1072 66 464

464/1072: Anṣārī suffered severe illness, but recovered. His sight was constantly weakening.

465/1072: Alp Arslān died. Mālik Shāh I, was 18 years old. Niẓām-al-Mulk administered all affairs of the empire.

The death of Abū'l-Qāsim al-Qushayrī, author of the "Risala on Sufism" in Nishāpūr.

467/1075: Al-Muqtadī was the Caliph in Baghdād.

468/1076: the Seljuqs defeated the Fatimids and conquered Damascus.

1076 70 469

He continued, during all these years, his teaching of Ḥadīth, Quranic commentary (tafsīr), and Sufism.

470/1078: 'Abd-al-Raḥmān ibn Manda died in Iṣfahān, a Hanbalite shaykh who exchanged letters with Anṣārī.

471/1079: Abū Ḥāmid al-Ghazzāli of Tūs was twenty years old.

1080 74 473

473/1080: Anṣārī *went blind.* He continued to dictate his lessons of tasfīr and Sufism. Very young students served as scribes: 'Abd-al-Awwal Sejzī, 'Abd-al-Mālik Karrokhī, Muḥammad Ṣaydalānī.

Ḥosayn Kotobī, his secretary, took care of his everyday life.

Anṣārī dictated to young novices the "Stations of the

Wayfarers" (Manāzil al-Sā'irīn), the famous manual
of Sufism in Arabic.
474/1082: The Caliph al-Muqtadī sent another robe
of honor to Anṣārī and called him
"Shaykh al-Islām" (The Senior of Islam).

I. Ages 79 to 82: The Battles of the Last Years (1085 - 1088 C.E.)

1085 79 478

Ramadhān 478/Dec. 1085: A philosophizing scholar of Kalām, who had entered Herāt, was severely criticized by Anṣārī. His followers burnt down the Kalāmī's house and beat him. Anṣārī and his companions were exiled and ordered to go to Balkh.
479/April 21, 1087, triumphant welcome at Herāt. Anṣārī continued the teaching of Quranic commentary.

1089 82 481

22 Dhū'l-Ḥijja 481, Friday, March 8, 1089:
Death of 'Abdullāh Anṣārī of Herāt. Buried on a rainy day at Gāzar=gāh near the Khānaqāh and the tomb of Shaykh 'Amū. Since then, Anṣārī's tomb has been a shrine for pilgrims.

Appendix B

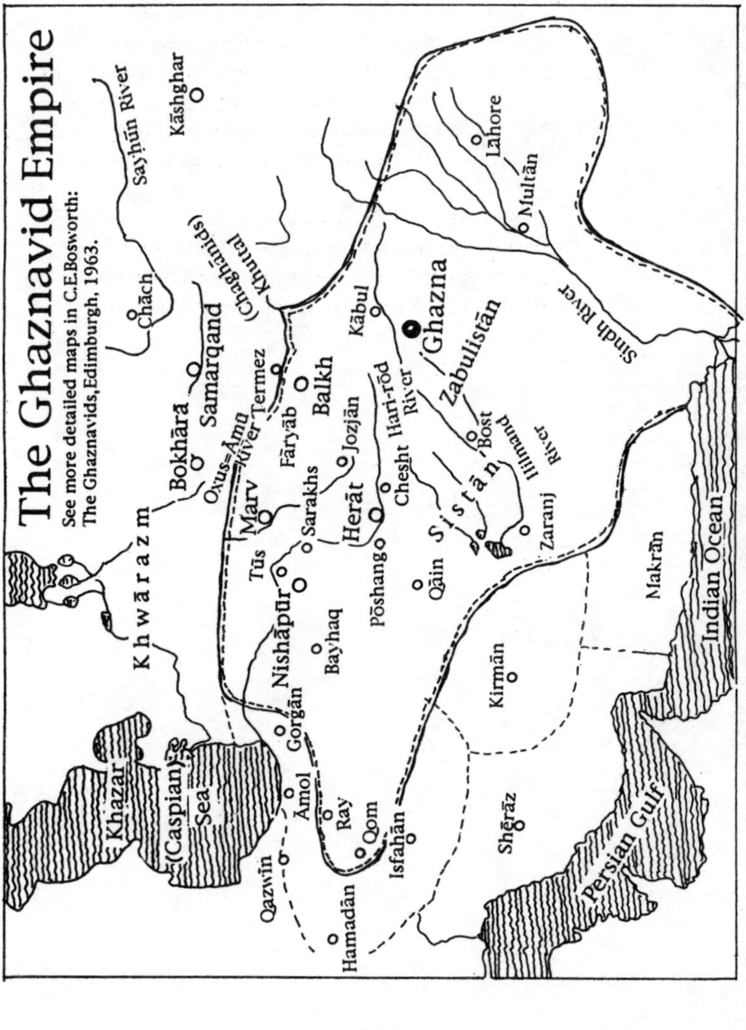

Map of the Ghaznavid Empire during the age of 'Abdullāh Anṣāri

Appendix C

CONCORDANCE OF TITLES OF SPIRITUAL STATIONS
Between "Stations of the Wayfarers", "Hundred Grounds", & "Flaws in the Stages"
of 'Abdullāh Anṣārī

Station Number in "Stations of the Wayfarers"	Arabic	English	Comparison to the Number in "Hundred Grounds"	Comparison to the Number in "Flaws in the Stages"
		I. Section of Beginnings (Bidāyāt)		
1	Yaqẓah	Awakening	12	
2	Tawbah	Repentance	1	
3	Muhāsabah	Appraisal	11	
4	Inābah	Turning (to Him)	3	
5	Tafakkur	Reflection	29	
6	Ta<u>dh</u>akkur	Self-Admonition	30	
7	I'tiṣām	Holding Fast	81	
8	Firār	Escape	42	
9	Riyāḍah	Austerity	9	
10	Samā'	Listening	87	
		II. Section of the Doors (Abwāb)		
11	Ḥuzn	Sorrow	x[1]	5, 11
12	<u>Kh</u>awf	Fear	33	6, 11
13	I<u>sh</u>fāq	Apprehension	36	
14	<u>Kh</u>u<u>sh</u>ū'	Humility	37	
15	I<u>kh</u>bāt	Serenity	39	
16	Zuhd	Renunciation	13	2, 11
17	Wara'	Abstaining	15	
18	Tabattul	Devotion	26	
19	Rijā'	Hope	43	7, 11
20	Rag<u>h</u>bah	Aspiration	45	

III. Section of Behaviors (Mu'amalāt)[2]

21	Ri'āyah	Watchfulness	50	
22	Murāqabah	Heedfulness	53	
23	Ḥurmah	Respect	57	
24	Ikhlāṣ	Sincerity	25	
25	Tahdhīb	Correction	10	
26	Istiqāmah	Perseverance	28	
27	Tawakkul	Trust (in God)	21	3, 11 (3)
28	Tafwīḍ	Reliance	66	
29	Thiqqah	Confidence	64	
30	Taslīm	Submission	79	

IV. Section of Virtues (Akhlāq)

31	Ṣabr	Endurance	7	4, 11 (4)
32	Riḍā'	Contentment	23	
33	Shukr	Thankfulness	x	8, 11 (8)
34	Ḥayā'	Decency	63	
35	Ṣidq	Truthfulness	61	
36	Ithār	Preference	65	
37	Khuluq	Character	x	
38	Tawāḍu'	Modesty	32	
39	Futuwwah	Generosity	4	
40	Inbisaṭ	Expansion	86	
41	Qaṣd	Aspiration	6	
42	'Azm	Resolution	27	
43	Irādah	Will	5	1, 11 (1)
44	Adab	Seemliness	55	
45	Yaqīn	Certitude	19	
46	Uns	Intimacy	95	
47	Dhikr	Remembrance	x	
48	Faqr	Poverty	31	
49	Ghinā'	Wealth	84	
50	Maqām al-Murād	Stage of Being Elected	x	

VI. Section of the Valleys (Awdiyya)

51	Iḥsān	Excellence	54
52	'Ilm	Knowledge	71
53	Ḥikmah	Wisdom	74
54	Baṣīrah	Insight	20
55	Firāsah	Perspicacity	x
56	Ta'ẓīm	Veneration	x
57	Ilhām	Inspiration	x

58	Sakīnah	Soothing	51	
59	Ṭuma'nīhah	Appeasing	52	
60	Himmah	Endeavor	49	

VII. Section of (Spiritual) States (Aḥwāl)

61	Maḥabbah	Love	101	9, 11 (9)
62	Ghayrah	Jealousy	58	
63	Shawq	Longing	x	10, 11 (10
64	Qalaq	Anxiety	x	
65	'Aṭsh	Thirst	x	
66	Wajd	Ecstasy	89	
67	Dahash	Alarm	96	
68	Haymān	Bewilderment	x	
69	Barq	Lightning	x	
70	Dhawq	Taste	x	

VIII. Section of Guardianships (Wilāyāt)

71.	Laḥẓa	Glance	90	
72	Waqt	Instant	91	
73	Ṣafā'	Purity	62	
74	Surūr	Delight	94	
75	Sirr	Secret	83	
76	Nafas	Breath	92	
77	Ghurbah	Exile	68	
78	Gharaq	Submersion	x	
79	Ghaybah	Absence	x	
80	Tamakkun	Establishment	56	

IX. Section of Realities (Ḥaqā'iq)

81	Mukāshafah	Unveiling	93	
82	Mushāhadah	Contemplation	97	
83	Mu'āyanah	Observation	98	
84	Ḥayāt	Life	73	
85	Qabḍ	Grasping	x	
86	Basṭ	Stretching	85	
87	Sukr	Intoxication	x	
88	Ṣaḥw	Lucidity	x	
89	Ittiṣāl	Association	x	
90	Infiṣāl	Disassociation	x	

X. Section of Fulfillments (Nihāyāt)

91	Ma'rifah	Knowing	75	

92	Fanā'	Annihilation	99
93	Baqā'	Subsisting	100
94	Taḥqīq	Realization	x
95	Talbīs	Covering	x
96	Wujūd	Finding	x
97	Tajrīd	Casting Aside	14
98	Tafrīd	Isolating	70
99	Jam'	Concentration	59
100	Tawḥīd	Unification	69

NOTES

1. The symbol "x" indicates names of stations in the "Stations of the Wayfarers" that had no precendent in the "Hundred Grounds".
2. Some of the stages mentioned in the "Hundred Grounds" became titles of sections and subsections in the "Stations of the Wayfarers" in plural forms: Behaviors, Guardianships and Realities.

GENERAL NOTE

The English translation of the names of the Stations is based on the text of Ansari, and in some cases is not in conformity with modern Arabic usage.

BIBLIOGRAPHY

Ansari, Abdullah, "The Invocation of Sheikh Abdullah Ansari", translated by Jogendra Singh, 3rd ed., London, 1959. (Based on later manuscripts).

Ansari, Abdullah, "Munājāt : The Intimate Prayers of Khwājih 'Abd Allāh Anṣārī" (based on later manuscripts of the "Invocations"), translated by Lawrence Morris and Rustam Sarfeh, New York Khanegah and Maktab of Maleknia Naseralishah, 1975.

Ansari, Abdullah, "Intimate Conversations," translated by W. Thackston (this translation is based on later manuscripts, specifically, a Persian text of a Tehran lithographic edition, n.d.); it is the second part of the book, in the "Classics of Western Spirituality" series, preceded by a preface by Annemarie Schimmel (and a translation from Arabic of Ibn 'Aṭa'llāh's "Book of Wisdom" by Victor Danner), New York : Paulist Press, 1978.

Anṣārī, "Cris du Coeur, Munâjât" (based on early manuscripts), translated (from Dari-Persian into French) by Serge de Laugier de Beaurecueil (cf. bibliography of his other Ansarian studies, p. 153), Paris : Sinbad 1988.

Anṣārī, "Chemin de Dieu" (the "Hundred Grounds," the "Stations" and "Flaws of the Stages" of 'Abdullāh Anṣārī) translated (from Arabic and Persian into French, with bibliography) by Serge Laugier de Beaurecueil, Paris: Sinbad, 1985.

Ansari, Abdullah, "Sad Maidan, Hundred Fields between Man and God,"translated from Persian to English, (but lacks accuracy and fidelity to the original text) by Munir Ahmad Mughal, Lahore : Islamic Book Foundation, 1983.

Beaurecueil, Serge de Laugier de, "Khwâja Abdullâh Ansâri (396-481 H./1006-1089), Mystique Hanbalite", Rocherches d'Institut de Lettres Orientales de Beyrouth, XXVI, Beirut : 1965. (in French)

Beaurecueil, Serge de Laugier de : edition and translation into French of the original Persian text of the "Sad Maydân", in "Mélanges Islamologiques", t. 2 (Cairo : IFAO, 1954), pp. 1-90; "Kitâb Manâzil al-Sa'irin, avec étude de la tradition textuelle, traduction, lexique" (Cario: IFAO, 1962) "Kitab 'ilal al-maqâmât" (ed. et trad.) in "Mélanges Massignon" (Damscus : 1956), pp. 153-71.

Beaurecueil, Serge de Laugier de, "Abdullāh al-Ansāri al-Haravi", article in "Encyclopaedia Iranica" (see the bibliography in the article). Vol: I, 1985 pp 186-190.

Beaurecueil, Serge Laugier de, "al-Ansāri al-Harawi", in "Encyclopedia of Islam, Second Edition.

Beaurecueil, Serge de Laugier de: Three articles translated into English : "Abdullāh Ansāri : A profile, Studying Ansari of Herat" (Conference at Sorbonne, 1971); "The Structure of Ansari's Book of Stages' (Manāzil us-Sāyerin)" together with "Abdullah Ansari and other Sufis of Afghanistan" (in the special issue of "Afghanistan Journal," April 1976, Historical Society of Afghanistan, Kabul, pp. 13-27).

Farhādi, A.G. Ravan, "The Hundred Grounds of Abdullāh Ansāri" (includes English translations of a few chapters of "Sad Maydān, together with some other chapters also contained in this book), in "Classical Persian Sufism : From Its Origins to Rūmi", edited by Dr. Leonard Lewisohn, Khaniqāh-i Nimatullāhi Publications London, 1993, pp. 381-399.

Arabic and Persian sources, books, and articles

Anṣārī, 'Abdullāh, "Tafsīr Kashf al-Asrār was 'uddat al-abrār" (Commentary on Qur'an, edited and expanded by Rashīd al-Dīn Maybodī), edited by 'Alī Aṣghar Ḥikmat, 10 vols. (Tehrān : Intishārat-i Danishgāhī, 1952-1960, reprinted subsequently).

Anṣārī, 'Abdullāh, "Ṭabaqāt al-Ṣūfiyya" : There are two published editions, ed. by 'Abd al-Ḥayy Ḥabībī (Kābul, 1961, reprinted in Tehrān, 1980) and by Muḥammad Sarvar Mawlāyi (Tehrān: Tus Pub, 1983) — the latter is obviously an improved edition.

Anṣārī 'Abdullāh, "Manāzil al-Sayerīn", "'Ilal al-Maqāmāt", (Arabic text with Persian translation), and "Sad Maydān" (Darī-Persian text) with an explanatory chapter and comparative lists of contents in Persian, 545 pages, by 'Abdul-Ghafūr Ravān Farhādī, Kābul : Bayhaqī, 1971; reprinted by Mawlā ed. Tehrān, 1982.

Anṣārī, 'Abdullāh, "Sokhanān-é Pīr-é Herāt", ed. by Muḥammad Jawād Sharī'at, 260 pages [pp. 77-188 contain "Sayings" and "Invocations" (munājāt) of Anṣārī extracted from the Kashf al-Asrār], Tehrān : 1976, Third Edition 1982.

Anṣārī, 'Abdullāh, "Munājāt-o Goftār-é Pir-é Herāt" (contains extracts from Kashf al-Asrār and from the Ṭabaqāt), ed. by Muḥammad Asef Fekrat, Kābul : Bayhaqī, 1976.

Anṣārī, 'Abdullāh, "Munājāt-é Khwāja 'Abdullāh Anṣārī", selected (from Kashf al-Asrār and Ṭabaqāt al-Ṣūfiyya) by Sabz-'Alī 'Alī-Panāh (nasta'līq calligraphy by Kayā'ī), 319 pages, Forūghī Ed., Tehrān : 1989.

Anṣārī,'Abdullāh, "Rasā'il-é Jāme'-é 'Āref-é Qarn-é Chahārom-é Hejrī, Khwāja 'Abdullāh Anṣārī" (mainly based on later manuscripts), ed. by Waḥīd Dastgardī (in Persian), 3rd ed., Tehrān: 1970.

Anṣārī, 'Abdullāh, "Rasā'il-é Khwāja 'Abdullāh Anṣārī" (mainly based on later manuscripts), ed. by Tābenda Gonābādi, Tehrān: n.d.

Anṣārī, 'Abdullāh, "Rasā'il-é Khwāja 'Abdullāh Anṣārī" (mainly based on later manuscripts), ed. by Muḥammad Shirwānī, Tehrān : Bonyād-é Farhang, n.d.

Jāmī, 'Abd-al-Raḥmān (d. 1492 C.E.), "Nafaḥāt al-Uns" : edition by Maḥmūd 'Ābedī, publ. by Enteshārat Mo'assessa Ettela'at, Tehrān : 1991. (last and best edition; many indexes).

Jāmi, 'Abd-al Rahmān (ed. Arberry, A.J.) "Manāqib Shaykh-al-Islām", in the "Islamic quarterly", 1963 p.p.57-82.

Beaurecueil, Serge de Laugier de, "Sargozasht-é Pir-é Herāt" ("The Life of 'Abdullāh Anṣārī"), translated from French into Persian by Ravān Farhādī, Kābul : Bayhaqī, 1971; reprinted by Mawlā ed., Tehrān, 1982.

Ba<u>sh</u>īr Hérawī, 'Alī-Aṣ<u>gh</u>ar, "Maqāmāt-é <u>Kh</u>wāja 'Abdullāh Anṣārī" (a biography of Anṣārī in Persian), Kābul : Ministry of Culture, 1976.

Farhādī, A.G. Ravān, "<u>Sh</u>enāsāyī-é Sad Maydān" (a survey of the Hundred Grounds; an article in Persian), in "Ṣūfī", Spring 1993 issue, London.

Sharī'at, Jawād, "Fehrest-é Tafsīr-é Ka<u>sh</u>f al-Asrār" (a general index of the "Commentary on the Qur'an"), Tehrān, 1984.

Abū-Manṣūr al-Isfahānī, "Nahj al-<u>Kh</u>āṣṣ, ("La Voie du Priviligié"), edited by S.L. de Beaurecuil, in "Mélanges Ṭāhā Ḥusayn", Cairo : 1962.

Khorram-Shāhi, B.: Quranology, a Collection of Essays on Quranic Topics (in Persian), Nahsr-é Mashriq (p.p. 176-178. are about Kashf al-Asrār)

Rokni, M. Mahdi: Latāyef-é az Qurān-e Karīm, Meshed, 1986 (Contains a part of the Kashf al-Asrār besides an analysis in Persian of the Quranic Commentary).

Introductory Books on Islamic Sufism

Haeri, Shaykh Fadhlallah, " The Elements of Sūfīsm", Element Books, Great Britain, 1986.

Lings, Martin, "What is Sūfīsm ?"
University of California Press
Berkeley, California, 1975, 1977.

Schimmel, Annemarie, "Mystical Dimensions of Islam", University of North Carolina Press, 1975.

Valiuddin, Dr. Mir, " The Quranic Ṣūfīsm", Motilal Banarasidass, Delhi, 1959, 1977.

NAME INDEX